The
Santa Barbara
County Courthouse

The Santa Barbara County Courthouse

**Patricia Gebhard
and Kathryn Masson**

Photographs by James Chen

2001 · Daniel & Daniel, Publishers
Santa Barbara, California

Acknowledgments

We gratefully acknowledge photographer James Chen for his incredible ability to turn pictures that chronicle the courthouse into works of art. His fine work does this magnificent building justice.

We also thank our publisher, John Daniel, and designer, Eric Larson, for their expertise and enthusiasm for this publication.

We especially thank Peggy Hayes, who cares about the building probably more than anyone and whose constant vigilance for more than twenty years has been a guiding force in its preservation.

Our deep thanks also go to a handful of Santa Barbarans, historians and people knowledgeable about the courthouse, who recounted legends and anecdotes, explained design details, and shared their feelings about this beloved building. Many of these people have spent countless hours and even years devoted to maintenance and preservation of the courthouse and have made it possible for thousands of visitors each year to appreciate this spectacular building. Others have helped this publication by their personal support of our work. We gratefully acknowledge the following:

Cameron Airhart, David Bisol, Norman Caldwell, Regula Campbell, John and Gloria Carswell, Hal Conklin, Michael Crowe, Oswald Da Ros, Mary Lousie Days, David Debs, Tony Heinsbergen, Jarrell C. and Michele Jackman, Carol Kenyon, Henry Lenny, Marilyn McMahon, Birdie Masson, Shauna Mika, Mayor Harriet Miller, Virginia Paca, Lex Palmer, David Pashley, John Pitman, Michael Redmon, Benjamin Sawyer, Matt and Beth Thomas, and members of the Courthouse Docent Council.

Published by Daniel & Daniel, Publishers, Inc.
Post Office Box 21922
Santa Barbara, CA 93121
www.danielpublishing.com

LIBRARY OF CONGRESS CATALOGING-IN-PUBLICATION DATA
Gebhard, Patricia.
    Santa Barbara County Courthouse / By Patricia Gebhard and Kathryn Masson.
        p.   cm.
    Includes bibliographical references.
    ISBN 1-880284-45-6 (pbk. : alk. paper)
    1. Santa Barbara County Courthouse (Santa Barbara, Calif.)   2. Architecture, Spanish colonial—
California.   3. Santa Barbara (Calif.)—Buildings, structures, etc.   I. Masson, Kathryn.   II. Title.
    NA4473.S25 G43 2001
    725'.15'0979491—dc21   00-010249

10 9 8 7 6 5 4 3 2 1

To David Gebhard
(1927–1996)

who loved Santa Barbara
and was a diligent and dedicated
educator and preserver of its integrity

Contents

Introduction : 11

COURTHOUSE HISTORY : 15
    Earlier Courthouses, 1850–1925 : 15
    The Competition for a New Courthouse : 17
    The Effect of the Earthquake : 18
    Creating Santa Barbara in a Spanish Image : 19
    The Planning of the New Courthouse : 21
    William Mooser and Company : 21
    Development of the Courthouse Design : 23
    Funding of the Building : 24
    Completion of the New Courthouse : 26
    Additions and Remodels : 26
    The Future of the Courthouse and Its Preservation : 27

THE EXTERIOR : 29
    Layout of the Courthouse : 30
    The Hall of Records Building : 31
    Giovanni Antolini, Master Stonecutter and Mason : 31
    Commemorative Plaques : 32
    The Entry and Doors of the Hall of Records : 33
    Albert Yann, Metal Artist : 34
    The Service Building : 34
    The Main Arch—Anacapa Street : 35
    The "Spirit of the Ocean" Fountain and Sculptor Ettore Cadorin : 36
    The Main Entrance Stonework : 37
    The Clock Tower : 38
    Clock and Carillon : 38
    Anacapa Wing : 40
    Cast-Stone Decoration : 43

Garden Façade and Circular Stair Tower : 44
Ironwork and Other Metalwork : 45
Courtrooms Building—Figueroa Wing, Garden Façade : 47
Courtrooms Building—Figueroa Wing, Figueroa Street Façade : 48
The Jail Wing : 50
Landscaping and the Sunken Gardens : 54

THE INTERIOR : 59
The Mural Room : 61
Dan Sayre Groesbeck, Muralist : 63
Description of the Murals : 64
Giovanni Battista Smeraldi, Artist : 67
The Law Library : 72
Tile : 74
Chemla Tile : 75
Les Fils de Chemla : 77
Gladding, McBean Tile : 78
Gladding, McBean and Company : 79
La Fitte Tile : 80
New Tile : 81
Tile Plaques : 81
The Corridors : 83
Doors : 85
Furniture : 85
Paintings : 87

Postscript : 91

Bibliography : 93

The
Santa Barbara
County Courthouse

Introduction

THE CURRENT SANTA BARBARA COUNTY COURTHOUSE, set near the center of town amid low, pedestrian-level buildings and surrounded by hillsides cascading with white-washed, red-tile-roofed buildings, presents itself as a grand palace rather than a utilitarian public building. Yet it captures all of the charm inherent in the vernacular architecture of Andalusian Spain in its seemingly haphazard combination of parts.

As the epitome of the Spanish colonial revival idiom, this courthouse, completed in 1929, represents a unique contribution to public architecture in the United States. Praising it beyond its stylistic limits, Charles Moore, an influential architect of the twentieth century, considered it one of the major buildings "on the planet." The design expresses on a magnificent scale the desire of Santa Barbara citizens to recreate Santa Barbara as a romantic Spanish city. Even its architect, William Mooser, claimed the courthouse was more Spanish than any hotel-de-ville in Spain.

An elite group of civic-minded Santa Barbara citizens not only chose the Spanish image as an appropriate style for a city with a Spanish past, but mandated its use in the courthouse. Even today, like-minded citizens have continued to insist on what might be called "the Santa Barbara style" in the downtown area through legislation and the establishment of a watchdog review committee.

By the 1920s, interest in and enthusiasm for the romantic, exotic, and picturesque elements of Spain, developed over the past decades, was at its height. Although travelers had written about their visits to Spain since the early nineteenth century, the book that popularized Moorish Spain was Washington Irving's *The Alhambra*, first published in 1832, republished in 1857, and again in 1896, with evocative illustrations by Joseph Pennell. The Alhambra and adjacent Generalife, Granada's magnificent fortress-palaces, exemplified the exotic sophistication of Moorish architecture as a culmination of a developed aesthetic more than any other buildings in Spain. Built and refurbished over time, the multiple buildings and gardens blend in perfect harmony on a hilltop in a vast landscape. The relationship of the interior and exterior spaces and the rich decoration in intricate plaster and tile provided an inspiration and impetus for Moorish designs in America.

However, accounts of Spanish art and architecture would not have been persuasive enough for California architects to espouse a Spanish-Mediterranean style if the United States as a whole had not been searching for a national style. The American colonial revival was born after the Philadelphia centennial of 1876, and American architects on the eastern seaboard sought to popularize colonial styles for domestic architecture nationwide. They were reasonably successful in their promotion. Colonial architecture flourished in the eastern states, and in the 1930s became the predominant domestic style throughout much of the United States.

At the end of the nineteenth century, architects in California found a basis for a regional style, the mission revival, in the provincial Spanish missions still in existence there. As part of this emulation of mission architecture, Californians began to work for the preservation of the extant missions and adobe buildings throughout the state. The mission revival style then evolved into the Spanish colonial revival, more accurately called Mediterranean revival, in the mid-teens and twenties, when the simplicity and austerity of the California missions were combined with more formal and ornate renaissance and baroque design elements from churches built in the American Southwest, Mexico, and Spain. In many of these churches elaborate churrigueresque plasterwork contrasted with planar façades of white stucco.

With major buildings designed by Bertram G. Goodhue using churrigueresque elements, the Panama–California Exposition of 1915 in San Diego put the stamp of approval on the use of these Spanish forms. However, a simpler Spanish expression based on the provincial buildings of Spain and Italy also emerged at that time. In Santa Barbara, architect George Washington Smith developed a less pretentious and more informal architectural style. Incorporating these two styles, the high art and the vernacular, the Spanish colonial or Mediterranean revival became the "California style" and locally came to be labeled the "Santa Barbara style."

By the 1920s, very little remained of the "real" past of Santa Barbara and its Spanish heritage. Only two significant structures survived: the mission, established in 1786 and completely reconstructed in 1812–1820, and the guardhouse, El Cuartel, of the original Spanish fort, El Presidio Royal. However, of the more than one hundred small adobe houses dating from the early nineteenth century clustered around the presidio in the original center of town, most had been demolished by the 1940s to make room for "progress." Today fewer than twenty remain. Yet these remnants of Santa Barbara's Spanish past provided the rationale upon which the city was remodeled in an authentic Spanish style.

By the late teens, the citizens of Santa Barbara had determined they wanted a Spanish-style courthouse, but favored the Spanish renaissance architecture of the exposition in San Diego. With the impetus of a group of displaced easterners recently enamored of Santa Barbara, the citizens devoted themselves to the cause of planning for the city's continued beauty and its re-creation in a uniform Spanish style. The earthquake of 1925 provided the opportunity not only to refashion the city as they desired, but also to erect a new courthouse.

In Santa Barbara, architects George Washington Smith, Winsor Soule, Carleton Winslow, Sr., James Osborne Craig, and Reginald D. Johnson were pioneers in embracing the Mediterranean style. Their widely published, appreciated, and imitated building designs provided models throughout California and the United States. Their work excelled due to their acquaintanceship with and sophisticated appreciation of Spanish and Mexican architecture, acquired through extensive travel and familiarity with historic and current literature.

Whether or not it is the country castle that architectural historian David Gebhard has labeled it, there is no question that the Santa Barbara County Courthouse is one of the finest public examples of the Spanish-Mediterranean style. Yet it is so idiosyncratic in its design that it can be admired and appreciated without reference to its Spanish

colonial revival stylistic designation. It is a delightfully bewildering medley of thick white walls and red-tiled roofs, unexpected stairwells and towers, graceful arches and balconies, charming windows and gates with iron grilles. The simple lines with long reaches of restful walls inside and out complement the lavish use of ornament. The white walls of the building provide a man-made contrast to the lush planting, which creates constantly shifting shadow patterns on the walls. It is the total ambiance of the buildings set in the now-mature, park-like landscape envisioned over seventy years ago that makes the courthouse so exceptional.

Much of the courthouse may still be enjoyed as it was originally conceived. The majority of the exterior, the lobbies, the interior galleries, the law library, and the Mural Room have remained unaltered since 1929, although some interior rooms have been remodeled over time. Accessible to the public, the Mural Room, no longer used for the county supervisors' meetings, remains the crowning glory of the building's interior, with its intricately painted walls and ceiling and its patterned tile floors.

Lauded in its own time as the city's greatest asset, the courthouse has received official recognition by its designation as a Santa Barbara city landmark and its placement on the National Register of Historic Places. It enhances the lives of all who have the good fortune to experience it and continues to impress inhabitants and visitors to Santa Barbara as one of the world's great architectural successes.

Courthouse History

When California became a state and Santa Barbara the seat of a county, space was needed for the new county's courts, offices, and jail. Santa Barbara County's population growth and accompanying increase in governmental services resulted in the use or erection of several different buildings, leading up to the building of the present county courthouse in 1929. Each new structure reflected the aesthetic taste of the time.

Earlier Courthouses, 1850–1925

In 1850, the first courts and county offices were located in the rented Aguirre adobe in the middle of downtown Santa Barbara on East Carrillo Street. Built in 1841 by Don Antonio Aguirre, its typical adobe plan was a group of single rooms, nineteen in this case, surrounding a large courtyard. Although made of adobe, it had a three-foot-thick stone foundation.

The Cota adobe became the second courthouse after the county purchased it in 1853. The county Grand Jury immediately found fault with this building, and it was replaced after only two years. The Cota adobe site was on Anacapa Street near the corner of Ortega Street.

With the purchase of the Kays adobe in 1855, the courthouse moved to its present site, flanked on four sides by Anacapa, Figueroa, Santa Barbara, and Anapamu streets. The low, spread-out Kays adobe was extensive in size and better fit the needs of the county. However, like the other adobes, it was difficult to maintain and particularly inadequate for use as a jail because prisoners could carve their way out through the adobe walls. But the main thing wrong with an adobe building, in the eyes of Yankee settlers, was its inability to present a monumental symbol of law and order for Anglos.

As early as 1866, the Grand Jury demanded a new building, finding the Kays adobe courthouse insufficient and too dilapidated for county services. In early

1872, a bill was passed in the California Senate and Assembly authorizing a new courthouse for Santa Barbara. The county considered a number of locations for the courthouse, finally settling on the Kays adobe site. The Board of Supervisors requested designs for the new building and selected Peter J. Barber as the architect. Barber was well known in Santa Barbara for his Arlington Hotel as well as numerous churches, schools, and commercial and residential buildings. The cornerstone of the new courthouse was laid October 7, 1872, and offices were occupied by early 1875. Bonds in the sum of $50,000 payable in 30 years at 7 percent were issued for the construction of the new courthouse. The building would contain the courtrooms and

judges' chambers as well as various county offices.

The new courthouse was built in a classical revival style, similar to that of many courthouses built at that time across the country, and represented a rejection of Santa Barbara County's Hispanic adobe tradition. The new building's floor plan was in the form of a Greek cross, and the entrance façade featured columns and a pediment. A small cupola with a dome covered the central space. Over the years the grounds were landscaped, so that by 1925 many trees and flowers embellished them.

Although this building remained in use as the courthouse until 1925, two substantial additions were required in order to accommodate growing needs. The first was an adjacent public records building. From among plans submitted, within a cost limit of $22,000, the supervisors chose that of architect Thomas Nixon, owner and operator of the Union Mill and Lumber Company. Nixon was a master carpenter and cabinetmaker who, in addition to designing the building, crafted the woodwork of the interior. The new public records building, shown opposite, was designed in the Queen Anne style, reflecting the town's enthusiasm for this late phase of Victorian architecture. It was fifty-two by sixty feet, had a forty-foot-high tower, and was considered to be a very fine building for its time (1889). However, it was built without thought for context, lacking harmony with the existing classical revival courthouse in its form and style.

Continued need for more space was answered in 1904–05 with expansion of the 1870s courthouse itself to provide larger courtrooms and offices. Designed by the Los Angeles firm of Train and Williams, this expansion basically filled in corners of the building, adding bays to each side delineated by classical pilasters.

The Competition for a New Courthouse

After World War I, both the 1875 courthouse and the public records building were considered inadequate, so that in early 1919 the county set in motion a competition for the design of a new courthouse. The structure was to be a war memorial and was to include an auditorium and offices for both the county and city governments.

The jury for the Santa Barbara County Courthouse and Memorial competition reviewed twelve entries and selected first through fourth place finalists on August 4, 1919. The first prize went to Edgar A. Mathews of San Francisco, whose entry (below) endeavored to create a Spanish theme in keeping with the history, culture, climate, and environment of Santa Barbara. William Mooser and Horace G. Simpson of San Francisco won second prize for a design (next page) that also reflected the Spanish antecedents of Santa Barbara.

Although this competition reflected a desire to build in the Spanish idiom and was an important prelude to the current courthouse, it did not result in the construction of a new building. The Spanish stylistic

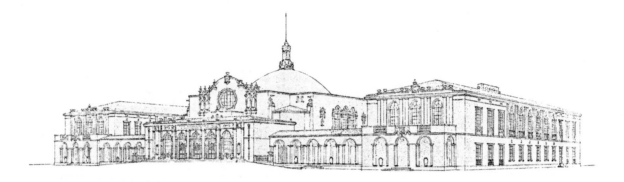

elements of the leading designs were formal, with elaborate decoration in Spanish renaissance or baroque style similar to buildings at the 1915 Panama–California Exposition in San Diego. None of the winning entries showed the simplicity of buildings in Andalusia favored by the citizens of Santa Barbara. It seems that the financial climate was not right for building the courthouse in 1919. The Board of Supervisors' minutes reported nothing further on the issue in the years immediately following the competition, and news articles since then have reported that it was because of "post-war shortages of materials and other readjustments" that the building was not built then. From the many bonds issued during these years, it is clear that the county was spending its funds on schools.

The Effect of the Earthquake

All of this changed dramatically on June 29, 1925, when an earthquake damaged both the courthouse and the hall of records. Both were beyond repair, making the erection of new buildings imperative. All of the philosophical jockeying, public opinions, preliminary public works codes, community committee work, and enthusiasm for the increasingly popular Spanish colonial revival style came together at that moment in history and provided Santa Barbara the best preparation it could possibly have had to conceive and construct a new and spectacular courthouse.

The earthquake struck at a time when Santa Barbara was already being envisioned in the Spanish image. City planning was well under way with completion of a comprehensive city plan in 1924 that is still used today. Also, fortuitously, in May 1925 the City Council had passed the Building Code Ordinance that set standards for construction. Immediately after the earthquake, a revision committee was set up to ensure that the ordinance reflected lessons learned from that experience, including proof of the strength of adobes and properly built concrete-and-steel construction. Such buildings withstood the force of the earthquake better than did post-and-beam and masonry buildings, providing another reason to reconstruct in concrete and stucco, which accommodated the Spanish style.

The county and city were able to establish committees and boards to address the problems of reconstruction in a Spanish idiom quickly because individuals and organizations had already been working on the replanning of Santa Barbara with that style in mind.

Creating Santa Barbara
in a Spanish Image

Bernhard Hoffmann was the most active leader in redesigning Santa Barbara in the Spanish style. When he arrived from New York in 1920, he immediately saw the importance of preserving Santa Barbara's architectural past and beautifying the city through planning and controlled building. When the Community Arts Association set up the Plans and Planting Committee in February 1922, Hoffmann became its chairman. Through the committee he advocated the restoration of local adobe structures and educated the public on the importance of Spanish design as a continuance of Santa Barbara's past.

Hoffmann believed that if the citizens of Santa Barbara were to become enthusiastic about rebuilding the town in the Spanish image, they must see it done effectively,

with groups of buildings together rather than single buildings scattered throughout the city. He led the way in this endeavor by purchasing and restoring the largest and most significant adobe in town, the Casa de la Guerra, and incorporating it into the first multi-use commercial complex in America, El Paseo (1922–24, James Osborne Craig, architectural designer; Mary Craig, designer; 1928–29, Carlton M. Winslow, Sr., architect). The El Paseo complex, entered through the Street of Spain opposite De La Guerra Plaza, was an immediate success both financially and aesthetically. It demonstrated how to incorporate the best aspects of traditional Spanish design in a modern building. A secluded interior courtyard with a central fountain surrounded by multi-level buildings with calming white-stuccoed walls, myriad passageways and terraces, heavy tiled roofs, rustic hand-wrought iron details, and semitropical plantings created an Eden in the middle of downtown.

Hoffmann also commissioned Meridian Studios (1922, George Washington Smith, architect) one block away from El Paseo, a courtyard complex that included the historic Lugo adobe, and his own residence near the mission, Casa Santa Cruz (1919–1922, James Osborne Craig, architectural designer), both in the Spanish style. In 1921 he organized an Architectural Advisory Committee to promote the redesign of De la Guerra Plaza and the design of the new City Hall (1922–23, Lockard and Sauter, architects) in a Mediterranean style.

Immediately after the 1925 earthquake, Hoffman resigned his post as chairman of the Plans and Planting Committee, turning its leadership over to Pearl Chase, and became chairman of the newly formed group then known as the Architectural Advisory Board. Although the Architectural Advisory Board included forty-two prominent citizens who volunteered their time and expertise, it was Hoffmann and two other professional men on the executive committee, architect T. Mitchell Hastings and attorney John M. Curran, who accomplished the major business of this policy-making body.

Responsible to the Board of Public Safety and Reconstruction and later to the City Planning Commission, the Architectural Advisory Board, at its first meeting, on July 7, 1925, recommended the establishment of an Architectural Board of Review. This board would review projects for code compliance and recommended changes in design, often referring projects to the Community Drafting Room for assistance. The Santa Barbara City Council appointed as members of the Architectural Board of Review Mr. Hoffmann, J.E. White (who was also chairman of the city Planning Commission), and three architects chosen for their leadership and skill in the design of buildings in the Spanish-Mediterranean style, George Washington Smith, Carleton M. Winslow, Sr., and William A. Edwards.

At the same meeting, the Architectural Advisory Board also established a design work center, the Community Drafting Room, providing an agency through which the Allied Architects of Los Angeles could assist the city of Santa Barbara in its rebuilding. Consulting architects in the Community Drafting Room offered design and drafting assistance at cost to architects and merchants for local projects. In the nine months following the earthquake, the Architectural Board of Review processed permits for more than 2000 buildings, a large number of which were designed and developed in the Community Drafting Room.

Further action of the Architectural Advisory Board included the adoption of a formal resolution recommending that the predominant style of façade treatment for business property be, as far as possible, in the "spirit of the California architectural tradition inherited by the city." This was one of the first architectural design codes in the United States. The Architectural Board of Review approved buildings that met code specifications and, more importantly, ensured that the designs were in the Spanish "Santa Barbara style." The remarkably swift rebuilding of Santa Barbara's downtown core was made possible by this coordinated community effort and a clear vision of style for reconstruction.

The Planning of the New Courthouse

A new county courthouse was on the top of the agenda when the County Board of Supervisors called a special meeting on July 3, 1925, four days after the earthquake. At this meeting the board set forth five design specifications regarding the building. These were that it face south, that it be built so that it might be multiplied by three or four without affecting the harmonious architecture, that the Hall of Records would be incorporated into the new design, that a county jail be a separate unit close to the courthouse, and that the style of architecture be Spanish renaissance, conforming to the style adopted in other Santa Barbara buildings.

At the same meeting the Board of Supervisors commissioned William Mooser II, owner of the architectural firm William Mooser and Company, to prepare plans and specifications for the project. Mooser had been the second-prize winner in the 1919 design competition, and so it is something of a mystery why the first-prize winner, Edgar A. Mathews, was not chosen for the project in 1925. Mathews was still practicing in San Francisco at that time, and continued to do so until the early forties. There are notes in the 1919 jury's report on the results of the competition that help explain why Mooser was chosen in 1925.

An article from July 25, 1919, in the Los Angeles–based newsletter *Southwest Builder and Contractor* explained, "According to reports the members of the Board of Supervisors are not satisfied with the plans submitted as none conform to their ideas of the building that they desire. This is not at all surprising. Plans prepared in accordance with a fixed program are not likely to reflect individual ideas except of the persons who prepare them. Competitions seldom produce a satisfactory solution of any architectural problem. They are merely an aid to the selection of an architect who possesses the qualifications necessary to work out the real solution with a more intimate knowledge of all the problems involved.... No architect submitting a plan in competition expects his first design to fulfill all requirements. It is merely the basis for more exhaustive study and elaboration of the final plan." In a meeting on October 5, 1925, the Board of Supervisors clearly stated that they preferred Mooser's competition design.

William Mooser and Company

William Mooser and Company was a wise choice for this monumental project. Based in San Francisco, the firm was headed by William Mooser II, who had been trained as an engineer. He had inherited the firm in 1898 from his father, William Mooser I, a Swiss immigrant of the mid-nineteenth century, who had become a successful architect in San Francisco, had served as president of the San Francisco Architectural Society, and had established, in 1854, the architectural firm that was to last into the next century.

Mooser II, who was in his late fifties when he worked on the Santa Barbara County Courthouse project, was well rounded in the architectural field. His company had planned and been active in the construction of many houses and public and commercial buildings. Furthermore, the Board of Supervisors was impressed that William Mooser and Company was experienced in designing and building courthouse complexes. More prominent among its designs were court-houses for the northern California counties of Contra Costa, Nevada, Marin, Stanislaus, and Tuolumne, as well as hospitals, schools, and a masonic home. In San Francisco, the firm designed the tower building of Ghirardelli Square, the much-remodeled Grant-Geary Center, and the Haslet warehouses near the aquatic park. William Mooser II had also served as president of the San Francisco Chapter of the American Institute of Architects.

While Mooser II headed the business, his son, William Mooser III, became the key figure in the supervision of the Santa Barbara County Courthouse project. William Mooser III, with a reputation as a brilliant artist, was trained in architecture at the Ecole des Beaux-Arts in Paris and had traveled extensively in Europe. At the request of his father, he returned from living for seventeen years in Spain, Italy, and France to help in the family business. Though his father remained in San Francisco, Mooser III moved to Santa Barbara with his French wife and two children to manage the courthouse project. On location as the official representative of William Mooser and Company, he made daily decisions on all aspects of the design and construction from his general contracting office at 209 Anacapa Street.

Though the records are incomplete, it may be assumed that Mooser's architectural firm was run as others are, with Mooser II as head of the firm and its official representative attending important meetings in Santa Barbara. These would have included Board of Supervisors meetings in which the courthouse was discussed, as well as special meetings with local architects, the Arbitra-tion Committee, and the Citizens Review Committee. William Mooser II, as official spokesperson for the firm, wrote articles about the building for publications such as *Architect and Engineer* and Santa Barbara's *Morning Press*. Mooser III, with his indispensable personal knowledge of the elements of Spanish architecture, designed or selected many of the interior and exterior details for the building, presented the firm's plans and specifications to the review organizations and subcontractors, and supervised the construction.

Father and son, working as a team, endured the controversy, conflict, and negotiation with various county boards and community leaders to produce the final result. Their temperaments and wisdom in letting representatives from the county have so much input into the design development undoubtedly resulted in the project's ultimate completion and a better building.

Development of the Courthouse Design

With input from the community, the Mooser firm entirely redesigned the 1919 plan. As noted, the original concept did not conform to the growing consensus that Santa Barbara's buildings should resemble the informal architecture of rural Andalusia. The elder Mooser had met with the architects of Santa Barbara and the Architectural Board of Review as early as July 1925 to discuss the plans and specifications. By September 1925 so many conflicting design suggestions had been made and argued over that the Board of Supervisors appointed an arbitration board to resolve disagreements among the Mooser firm, the Architectural Board of Review, and the Board of Supervisors.

The newly formed Arbitration Board consisted of Frederick Forrest Peabody, George A. Batchelder, and G. Allan Hancock, all influential citizens and nationally prominent businessmen. George Batchelder became the chief negotiator and played a major role in the politics of the courthouse construction. His enthusiasm and expertise were crucial in the development of Santa Barbara and in building the courthouse in the Spanish style.

Batchelder, considered the "Father of the [Santa Barbara] Riviera," had retired from his banking business in 1908 and had moved to Santa Barbara, where he masterminded the plan of the foothill area facing the city. His vision for a Santa Barbara Riviera led him to create the winding roads along which home sites were generously plotted (his own residence on La Paterna was one of the first built, in 1914). He hired Italian masons to work native sandstone into the decorative but functional curbs, revetments, walls, gateposts, and steps that still stand today. The oak seedlings he planted have matured into foliage that enhances what were then sparsely vegetated hillsides, and his insistence that all utilities be placed underground allows an uncluttered view of the beautiful landscape.

In September 1925, with a tight deadline for cost estimates, which were needed for the November bond election, Batchelder asked J. Wilmer Hershey, a member of the Community Drafting Room, to make drawings for a modified design. Hershey's quick sketches, like the one shown on the following page, became the basis of the new and accepted courthouse design, reflecting the informal character of Andalusian Spain rather than high renaissance formality. Mooser said about the Hershey design, "The new plan around a central court thus took on that atmosphere of romantic Spain in which Santa Barbara had begun to appear before the world."

Although Mooser is listed as the principal architect, he credited Hershey for his design contribution in an article he wrote about the courthouse for the *Morning Press*. Trained in architecture at the Carnegie Institute of Technology and a consulting designer for the rehabilitation of Santa Barbara in the Spanish style, Hershey has been called the genius who produced the first sketch for the new Santa Barbara County Courthouse. His participation is evident in the payroll accounts kept by the Community Drafting Room. He was paid regularly from July through October 1925, but with a special payment made in October. He no longer appears on the payroll

ELEVATION · ON · ANACAPA · STREET ~
PROPOSED · COURT·HOUSE · FOR · SANTA BARBARA COUNTY

thereafter. Perhaps he was already failing in health, for he died the following year, only thirty-one years old. In the January 1928 edition of *California Southland*, Hershey was described as "...that beloved artist whose early passing deprived California of one of her most talented designers...."

While Hershey did make important contributions to the design, the major credit for the building must be given to the Mooser firm. The architects successfully completed the project and with adeptness, addressed the diverse concerns and personalities in the community, integrated conflicting ideas into a final beautiful design, prepared the final plans and working drawings, selected and paid careful attention to the installation of the materials, and supervised the construction. The latter included working with artisans whose fine craftsmanship made the building a work of art.

Funding of the Building

The Board of Supervisors planned to fund the new county courthouse through the sale of bonds. Scarcely a month after the earthquake, in July 1925, they began the process for a countywide bond election for construction, finalizing it in October of that year, when plans and specifications were accepted. The bond issue of $980,000, put to the vote in November of 1925, failed because of controversies over the design and budget. This did not deter the Board of Supervisors, who decided in January to proceed with the building of the courthouse with Mooser as the architect. At its February meeting the Board of Supervisors decided to appoint a large committee to review the plans and prevent further arguments over the design and costs. The committee would consist of five persons from each supervisorial district as well as State Senator J. James Hollister, Assemblyman E.O. Campbell, and Judge S.E. Crow, who was particularly concerned with costs. The committee reaffirmed that the courthouse would be unusual not only in style but also in economy of construction, addressing any concerns about the cost.

Even before the first bond election, it was decided that expensive materials normally used on civic buildings, such as polished brass, marble, and bronze, would not be used. Instead, plain plastered walls, cut Santa Barbara sandstone that was readily available, decorative tile, simple wooden furniture—even some recycled and refurbished from the former courthouse—and economical iron fixtures would be used. The authenticity and charm of the Spanish style would be enhanced by the simplicity of these materials. The committee also decided that instead of hiring a large, expensive general contracting firm, the different facets of the work would be bid on by local subcontractors, thereby saving money.

Taking into consideration the opinions and concerns of this committee, the local architects, and other interested parties, the Mooser firm revised the courthouse design and reduced its cost in order to make a new bond issue more attractive to voters. Photographs made of a new model were published in the newspaper for public review before the Mooser firm's final revised plan was formally accepted and approved, first by the committee and then by the Board of Supervisors in April 1926. The revised lower budget of $700,000 was also submitted, and the second bond election succeeded on June 15, 1926. The last payment on this bond was made in 1946.

Until the bond was passed, Mooser was paid out of the earthquake emergency fund. Afterwards, from the bond money, he was paid 6 percent for the design of the building, in installments and, later, 4 percent for superintendence and inspection.

The final cost of the building was $1,368,000. The balance of the money needed to complete the courthouse after the bond money in the "courthouse fund" was exhausted came from an unorthodox financial plan. This plan was inspired by then-chairman of the Board of Supervisors, Charles Leo Preisker, and masterminded by Supervisor Samuel J. Stanwood, the liaison between the supervisors and the architect during the period of construction.

Again, personality played an important role in the building of Santa Barbara. Samuel J. Stanwood, another forceful man on the scene at that time, enthusiastically endorsed the Spanish style for Santa Barbara and worked tirelessly and effectively for completion of the courthouse in that style. Elected to the Board of Supervisors in 1917 with the agenda of having his favorite horse trails graded to be used by automobiles, he remained in office for more than a quarter of a century. He headed the first and subsequent twenty-four celebrations of Old Spanish Days Fiesta as El Presidente. As a respected member of the Board of Supervisors, he was singled out to work with the architects on behalf of the board, which he did by using his considerable personal influence to keep the courthouse budget in the black.

The financial scheme, which Stanwood spearheaded and which made the completion of the courthouse possible by 1929, was based on fortuitous oil strikes in 1928 at the Ellwood fields to the northwest of Santa Barbara. Originally put into the "unbudgeted reserves" of the county general fund, the money, derived from tax revenues on the assessed value of the oil-bearing land, was transferred into the courthouse fund as needed. The wells ultimately yielded over one hundred million barrels of oil. The transfer of funds from the general fund into the courthouse fund allowed construction to continue non-stop from its commencement in October 1926 until completion in March 1929.

Since the actual cost of the project was well above the bond amount, there is no doubt that without the ingenious use of "oil money" the courthouse could not have been finished. Further excavation and substructure for vaults, the installation of plumbing for hot water, landscaping, all interior design including furnishings and fixtures, equipment, and fees had raised the actual costs.

Completion of the New Courthouse

The cornerstone was laid in August 1927 during the Old Spanish Days Fiesta, and the courthouse was completed and functional by March 1929. It was officially dedicated at the opening of Old Spanish Days Fiesta on August 14, 1929, with many festivities and much praise in a special edition of the local newspaper. All of the contractors who had worked on the courthouse took out special ads, many of them full-page, to promote their businesses and to show pride in their accomplishments. The architect praised many of the subcontractors as "co-artists." Starting with that newspaper issue and through the years in subsequent magazine articles and other media coverage, the building has received national and worldwide accolades for its architecture.

The synchronicity of events in Santa Barbara that made the building of the courthouse possible is almost eerie: the earthquake's devastation after the Spanish style was popularized and endorsed, the tremendous effort of so many people focused on reconstruction, the choice of such a competent architectural firm, the availability of so many trained European artists, the striking of oil in the county in 1928, and the courthouse's successful completion before onset of the Great Depression—all combined to make this ambitious project possible.

Additions and Remodels

Within thirty-five years of the beginning of the courthouse's use, the county administrative services had outgrown it and a new contemporary styled building was constructed in 1964–66 facing it across Anapamu Street. The new building is adequate, but does not elicit much enthusiasm or admiration. After many county services moved to the new building in 1967, the courthouse interior was remodeled to provide more courtrooms. Since then the interior was again remodeled and upgraded in 1973 and 1983, resulting in six Superior Court courtrooms instead of the original two. Portions of an attempted Danish modern remodel in 1959 remain intermixed with remnants of the 1929 interiors of the two original courtrooms. The Smeraldi-painted ceilings, some lighting fixtures, and portions of decorative velvet curtain-panels behind the judges' chairs only hint at the past grandeur of those chambers. The two original courtrooms, along with the other four courtrooms, now share an overall generic quality. The Mural Room (former Board of Supervisors' assembly room) remains preserved due to a decision made by the Board of Supervisors in 1974 that it would not be modified.

In 1991 a ten-million-dollar courthouse complex upgrade began. More interior remodeling took place, and the building was brought into compliance with federal requirements for handicapped accessibility. Charles W. Moore, FAIA, was chosen as the architect. He consulted with Rex Lotery of Urban Innovations Group of Los Angeles; Mahan and Lenny, architects, of Santa Barbara; and David Gebhard, architectural historian. Campbell and Campbell, landscape architects, architect and planners of Los Angeles and Santa Barbara, were hired as part of the design team to landscape paths and provide a long-term maintenance plan for all of the courthouse's landscaping. In 1998 a separate jury assembly and courtroom were built across Santa Barbara Street from the courthouse.

The Future of the Courthouse and Its Preservation

Citizens of Santa Barbara and especially the Docent Council of the courthouse maintain constant vigilance over the courthouse, dedicated to preserving its character and keeping it well maintained. The Docent Council works with the County Board of Supervisors to make the most pressing repairs and identify areas for future preservation focus. County funds as well as monies donated to the Docent Council help in myriad ways to maintain this tremendous asset.

The "All About the Courthouse Program" spearheaded by the Junior League of Santa Barbara, working in conjunction with the Lawyers Wives of the Santa Barbara County Bar Association, began docent courses in 1974 as a community project.

Under the leadership of Marilyn McMahon, who was commended for her effort by then-President Richard M. Nixon and presented with the Medal of the Excelsior, the first public tours were given by twenty founding docents to an enthusiastic 450 people on Law Day, May 1, 1974. The Santa Barbara County Courthouse Docent Council, Inc., grew out of this original training program and was incorporated in 1982 as a volunteer organization whose members are trained in the history and design details of the courthouse.

The Docent Council's members, especially Peggy Hayes, the courthouse's most dedicated preservation advocate for some twenty-three years and currently serving in a voluntary capacity as curator and archivist, deserve special thanks for all their work through the years at the courthouse. They have been responsible for preserving records, staffing the information center, guiding free tours, advising the Board of Supervisors on maintenance concerns, advocating in the community for special needs, raising needed funds for projects, and negotiating with specialists in their fields to do necessary work on this very unique structure. The legacy of citizen involvement with Santa Barbara's honored heritage continues.

DIOS · NOS · DIO · LOS · CAMPOS
EL · ARTE · HVMANA · EDIFICO · CIVDADES

The Exterior

The Victorian art and architecture critic John Ruskin, discussing the "possible virtues of architecture" in volume I of *The Stones of Venice*, explains that, "In the main, we require from buildings…two kinds of goodness: first, the doing their practical duty well; then that they be graceful and pleasing in doing it." "Strength and beauty," he continues, are the sources of virtue for both a building's "action" and its "aspect." The courthouse has stood well in doing its "practical duty" as a center for the governmental and judicial systems of the county and has unarguably been pleasing while doing it.

In the words of its architect, William Mooser, "The secret of the picturesqueness and beauty of the Santa Barbara courthouse is to be found in developing the structure and the various architectural effects to scale. In building the Santa Barbara courthouse we tried to get back to the massive scale of building as carried out by the Spaniards. In many instances a building excellently conceived is ruined because the design has been carried out in a smaller scale than was warranted." The monumental scale of the building masses of the courthouse in relation to the site, to each other, and to the cityscape as well as to the scale of individually designed decorative elements show how effectively Mooser achieved this goal.

The Santa Barbara County Courthouse is a potpourri of Spanish architectural elements held together by the overall concept of its design. The vast blank wall spaces surrounding particular and often ornate ornamental applications create a simple, bold statement. The courthouse is a complex arrangement of thick, white walls, widely varying windows, loggias, galleries, and ornamental and architectural details. Because of its combination of disparate elements that make a coherent whole, renowned architect Charles W. Moore described it as "one of the century's great monuments to the architecture of inclusion."

This concept of making a whole out of

distinct building units makes the courthouse appear to be a village constructed over a period of time, like parts of the cities of Cordoba, Ronda, or Seville. Its encyclopedic inclusion of Spanish motifs reflects the enthusiasm of the architects of Santa Barbara for the Andalusian architecture of southern Spain, upon which the rebuilding of Santa Barbara was based. However, even before the rebuilding of the city after the 1925 earthquake, architects in Santa Barbara had developed sketches for redesigning State Street making use of this concept of separate units in a Spanish vernacular. Their designs for the façades of State Street, one block away from the courthouse, were planned with individualized Spanish forms for stores, banks, and restaurants, some with arcades, some with arched entries, but all with plain plastered walls and red-tile roofs.

The cohesion of design in the courthouse relies on similarity of materials and variation of design motifs rather than a balanced regularity or symmetry of forms. The consistencies that tie the courthouse together are design elements that comprise the Spanish-Mediterranean style. They include the use of thick, white-plastered walls, loggias, exterior staircases, towers, repetitive windows, iron grille work for windows, balcony railings, and gates, balconies, decorative tile and red-tile roofs. Variations exist in the treatment of rooflines, entrances, and windows, but the informal, haphazard arrangement of these elements create the total effect that is the main characteristic of the building.

Layout of the Courthouse

The courthouse with its surrounding gardens occupies an entire city block. It forms an uneven-sided "U" shape, with the interior open space a beautifully landscaped garden that becomes a lush park and functional community space. The planting and the sixty-foot setbacks from the streets mitigate the monumental scale of the building and provide an effective setting and views from many perspectives.

The courthouse consists of four structures, but because of exterior delineation it appears to be made up of more. The largest of these structures is the "L" shaped courtrooms building, with two "wings," one facing Anacapa Street and the other facing Figueroa Street (identified as the Anacapa wing and the Figueroa wing). On Anacapa Street at the far end of the "U" is the Hall of Records building, which also faces Anapamu Street. Adjacent to the Hall of Records is the service building, joined to the Anacapa wing of the courtrooms building by the main arch. At the other end of the "U," the jail section is joined to the Figueroa wing by an elevated bridge and corridor.

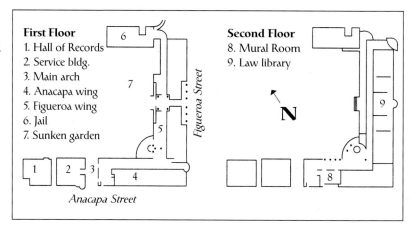

First Floor
1. Hall of Records
2. Service bldg.
3. Main arch
4. Anacapa wing
5. Figueroa wing
6. Jail
7. Sunken garden

Figueroa Street

Anacapa Street

Second Floor
8. Mural Room
9. Law library

N

The Hall of Records Building

The Hall of Records building functions today, as always, as the repository and office for marriage licenses, birth certificates, passports, real estate filings, and other legal documents and records of the county. Externally, the Hall of Records is a distinct entity to be admired by itself. The effectiveness of its design comes in large part from the expressive contrast between the decorative, honey-colored Refugio stone and the plain white walls. Oversized quoins of stone surround the doors and windows and Gothic arches of the entry. Elsewhere on the courthouse this same stonework is used at the base of the building and for structural and decorative motifs.

Giovanni Antolini, Master Stonecutter and Mason (1891–1975)

The sandstone used for all the courthouse stonework (except that of the fountain) was quarried at Refugio Canyon, a few miles north of Santa Barbara. It was installed under the direction of Giovanni Antolini.

Antolini was born in

Vestrano, Italy in 1891. After apprenticing under his father, a stonemason of considerable renown in his homeland, he worked in Switzerland, Germany, and France, before immigrating to the United States in 1912. He settled in Santa Barbara after spending a few months in Santa Maria learning English. As foreman for the architect Roland F. Sauter, he worked on various residential projects in Santa Barbara before opening his own company in 1922. Although he worked in other parts of the state, his best work is in Santa Barbara, including the Parish House of Trinity Episcopal Church and the Biltmore Hotel (Reginald D. Johnson, architect) in addition to the courthouse.

Antolini was the head stonemason of the courthouse in charge of installation, although Bly Stone Company of Los Angeles won the contract to quarry and prepare the stone. Antolini's crew numbered the massive blocks of sandstone at the Refugio Canyon quarry after skillfully working them with hand tools, then transported them to the construction site. Scaffolding and structures to hold the huge blocks were designed and built to allow proper setting of the stone pieces. Fine "cross-tooling" created a textural crosshatched effect on the surface of the stone blocks. The Antolini family carries on the tradition of stonework today in Santa Maria, California.

Commemorative Plaques

Three commemorative plaques, appearing almost as windows on the Anacapa Street façade of the Hall of Records building, mark visits of notable world figures to Santa Barbara. In 1929, the Mooser firm placed two of the plaques with the intention that these

embedded tiles would create the illusion that the building had already been standing for many years. One commemorates the visit of the King and Queen of Belgium in 1919, and the other the visit in 1914 of the fifteenth Count of Monterey, a descendent of the sixteenth-century count who commissioned the explorations of Viscaino, the explorer who surveyed the coast and named the channel for St. Barbara.

In 1983, a modern plaque was placed next to the other two. It commemorates the visit of Queen Elizabeth II and Prince Philip to Santa Barbara, and mentions then-president Ronald Reagan. Featuring the royal coat of arms surrounded by golden Tudor roses, it is the work of Santa Barbara ceramic artist Judith Sutcliffe.

as the Parador Conde of Gondomar of Bayona (Pontevedra), Spain. A Spanish pendant lantern of wrought iron and colored glass marks the corner of the building.

A stone path leads directly from the sidewalk through nineteenth-century stone gateposts to the low stairs and foyer of the Hall of Records building, where large exterior wood-and-copper doors protect smaller doors and the offices within. These gigantic entrance doors have the appearance of cathedral or castle doors. In accordance with Spanish tradition, massive, ornate doors often announce formal entrances. These monumental double doors tower thirteen feet in height and stretch eight feet across when closed. The designs on the copper plates were created by hammering from the backside of the copper piece, a method called "repoussé." The doors are among the most outstanding works of art on the courthouse's exterior. Rustic hand-wrought iron hardware and the iron studs that hold the thirty decorative copper pieces in place complement the wooden door frames.

Both the hand-tooled artistry and the stories that are told in each of these picture panels are significant. On each of the thirty individual copper pieces a separate picture

The Entry and Doors of the Hall of Records

The entry is unusual in its proportions, the subtleties of its scale, and its use of asymmetry. The entire corner of the building seems to rest on a short, thick column that supports low stone arches. It is similar in the relationship between its arched opening and the wall above to the building now used

depicts a symbol, a figure, or an allegorical scene of California and Santa Barbara history. These copper pieces are arranged in four columns or panels. When viewed as a whole, from a distance with the doors closed, they combine to present larger, bolder pictures, like larger puzzles made up of smaller pieces.

The plates in the far left column of the left door combine to depict the "tree of life." At the top of the next column to the right is a huge bird, an eagle that represents the state, a symbol used by early Spanish explorers. Columns three and four include a huge female figure (the Spirit of California) that continues through several plates. Individual plates throughout include the head of Saint Barbara, the figure of Father Junipero Serra, a scene of ships with Spanish and English explorers, padres and soldiers, forty-niners raising the "bear" flag during the 1849 gold rush, and the raising of the American flag by General Frémont, with pioneers, their covered wagons, miners, and prospectors.

Albert Yann, Metal Artist

Albert Yann of San Francisco executed the repoussé panels of the Hall of Records entry doors based on a design by San Francisco sculptor John MacQuarrie. Yann was born in Budapest in 1892 and was already noted as a gifted artist at the age of fourteen while working with French master metal-craftsmen at Prince Josef's palace in Austria. He came to the United States in 1918 seeking a more open political climate and more opportunity. Initially he settled in Los Angeles, where his commissioned works include copper relief, ornamentation, statuary, and busts that adorn many commercial and residential buildings. As a serious craftsman-artist he

created unique work in metal in an age of machinery and mass production. The copper relief doors of the Hall of Records are among his major works.

The Service Building

The service building declares itself as an entity separate from the adjacent Hall of Records by the open space between the buildings and by its completely different treatment of rooflines, windows, doors, grille work, and balconies. The regularity of its window treatment and the minimal detailing on this building complement the elaborate main arch to its right.

Originally the service building contained a number of non-elective offices and a drafting room, the Horticultural Commissioner, Farm Advisor, and Sealer, and an exhibition room on the first floor. The Health and Welfare Department was located on the second floor, and the County Surveyor and Planning and Map Department on the third. The Grand Jury was located over the main arch in a corridor leading to the main courtrooms building. The use of the offices has changed over the years. At present the Grand Jury, the offices for the general and facilities services of the county, and the purchasing office for the county are located in this building, with the Public Defender's office now over the arch. The space on the second floor includes a spacious conference room.

The service building appears as a townhouse on both façades, with an interesting wooden balcony on the garden side. The building has no evident entrances on either of its two main facades. Access is from the sides of the building, through an arched door in the "tunnel" of the main entry arch and via the ramp for handicapped users that also provides access to the Hall of Records. The entry within the main arch is a handsome wooden door with a Gothic-style lunette of turned wooden spindles, surrounded by hand-chiseled stone quoining. Above the door is a quatrefoil opening made up of lobes and cusps, whose shape represents an adaptation of the celestial form of a four-pointed star. It is typically used in Spanish colonial buildings in Mexico and the United States, but is not found in Spain. There are four occurrences of this shape of window in the courthouse. To the right of this door on the wall is a plaque honoring the supervisors at the time the building was erected, with a small grilled window next to it.

The Main Arch–Anacapa Street
The major focal point of the courthouse is the monumental entry arch on the Anacapa Street façade with the four-story tower, the fountain, and the view to the garden and distant hills beyond.

The courthouse arch is freely adapted from the Roman triumphal arch motif that was widely interpreted with varying elaborateness throughout Europe and particularly in Spain. For example, the House of the Carvajales in Caceres, pictured in Winsor Soule's *Spanish Farm Houses and Minor Public Buildings*, has an archway of this style in which the columns, medallions, and sculptured figures above the columns are placed in a similar location to those of the courthouse.

The smoothly carved columns with their Corinthian capitals and the moldings that define the main entrance arch contrast texturally with the oversized rusticated stone quoining that emphasizes this cavernous entry. The beautiful proportions of the high vault and large column bases, columns, and the decorative pediment that holds two eight-foot seated statues, disguise its enormous scale.

The "Spirit of the Ocean" Fountain and Sculptor Ettore Cadorin

The large stone fountain presents itself as an elaborate and enlarged base for the left-hand column supporting the main entry arch. Designed and sculpted by Ettore Cadorin (1879–1952), the courthouse's only fountain is entitled "Spirit of the Ocean." With its grouping of two wistful youths, it allegorically expresses the artist's conception of the Pacific Ocean, an integral part of Santa Barbara's history. Two local children, Maya Sexauer Seyer and her brother, posed for the figures.

This, as well as Cadorin's other masterpieces of stone sculpture on the exterior of the courthouse, including all of the figures on the triumphal arch, was done by the artist himself and by expert carvers under his direction. After having studied at the Royal Academy of Fine Arts and worked in Venice (his birthplace) and Paris, Cadorin was engaged to lecture on Italian literature and art at Columbia University in 1915. During that time in the United States, he exhibited in New York City and Boston, garnering commissions for bronze and marble statuary with favorable reviews by art critics. In 1917 he served in the war in Italy, but a year later was commissioned by the Italian government once again to lecture and organize official exhibitions of Italian art in the United States and of American art in Italy.

Cadorin was invited to exhibit his work in Los Angeles and Pasadena. From his California contacts, he received the invitation to work on the Santa Barbara County Courthouse. He set up a studio in Santa Barbara and was thereafter an active member of the art community as well as a teacher of art and drawing at the Santa Barbara State College. Other works by Cadorin in the United States include statues of the four apostles for the National Cathedral and the bronze statue of Father Junipero Serra in Statuary Hall in the Capitol in Washington

D.C. This statue was reproduced for the Old Plaza of Los Angeles in 1934.

Since the finely executed "Spirit of the Ocean" is particularly significant in the arch composition, it is unfortunate that, possibly for economic reasons, it was executed in inferior sandstone. Because of porosity problems inherent in the stone, it has weathered poorly. Costly reconstruction was done in the 1980s to abate deterioration, but the statue continues to need careful maintenance. Preservation efforts now include consultation with experts nationwide and a major fund-raising drive to ultimately contract for major repair or replacement.

The Main Entrance Stonework

The carved stonework surrounding the main arch incorporates varied architectural elements. To balance the fountain, a stone cartouche on the base of the right column contains a castle design found on the seal of the Board of Supervisors. The arch is crowned by a stone entablature, at the ends of which the statues of Justice and Ceres (the goddess of grain, harvest, and agriculture in Roman mythology) serve as gigantic finials. These huge statues, also the work of Ettore Cadorin, add drama to the arch as they sit in judgement over all those who pass through it. The entablature is inscribed with a Spanish translation of a phrase from the Roman scholar Varro's work, *De Re Rustica* (On Agriculture) that reads,

DIOS NOS DIO LOS CAMPOS
EL ARTE HUMANA EDIFICO CIUDADES

Originally a different phrase was to be inscribed in Latin. This is the only place on the courthouse where a Spanish inscription has been used, purportedly the idea of George Batchelder. An English translation of it is carved into the smaller archway over the doorway to the right of the grand arch and reads,

GOD GAVE US THE COUNTRY
THE SKILL OF MAN HATH BUILT THE TOWN
VARRO A.D. 50

Varro's original Latin phrase, as translated into English in John Bartlett's *Familiar Quotations*, reads, "Divine Nature gave the fields, human art built the cities." There is also a line in William Cowper's 1785 poem "The Task" that reads, "God made the country, and man made the town." A modern translation of the Spanish phrase on the courthouse is "God gave us the fields, human art built cities." The English inscription is, then, a paraphrased combination of all of these. The Varro date of A.D. 50, however, is incorrect, as he lived from 116–27 B.C.

The two carved stone medallions on triangular surfaces above the arch further honor the development of Santa Barbara's major industries. Agriculture is exemplified in one medallion with a bas-relief figure holding various fruits in one hand and a bunch of grapes in the other, with a decorative flock of sheep carved along the bottom of the circle. Transportation and industry are represented on the other medallion by a figure clutching electrical bolts (to represent the power of industry) in one hand and a ship in the other. A train runs along its lower edge.

The Clock Tower

Visible for blocks, the main tower, rising to a four-story height of 114 feet, is a defining feature of the courthouse. At the top, arched openings give access to a balcony protected by a decorative iron railing that completely surrounds the tower, providing the visitors with a 360–degree panoramic view of the city, foothills, and the islands across the Santa Barbara Channel. Viewers find their bearings with the aid of a bronze compass embedded in the floor.

Set asymmetrically above the Anacapa Street entry arch, the huge tower is square, as are many of the minarets of the Barbary Coast of North Africa, the area from which much of the Moorish architecture of Spain was derived. It is reminiscent of the towers in the garden of the Generalife in Granada and of one in a country church in Lorca. An extensive section on towers is found in Austin Whittlesey's *The Minor Ecclesiastical Domestic and Garden Architecture of Southern Spain*, a source that may have been used by the courthouse's designers. Using design features from other buildings does not deny the creativity of the architects, but indicates their awareness and knowledge of historic Spanish forms.

Clock and Carillon

Clock faces on all four sides of the tower originally had huge Roman numerals and clock hands made of solid oak. The clock was the city's largest timepiece. In 1964, when the hands on the ocean side of the tower froze in place, a check of the inner works found that the wood had rotted. New hands were commissioned and fashioned of marine plywood covered with fiberglass, using the old hands as patterns. With hands and numerals painted black, the clock faces can be read from a distance.

Original plans envisioned bronze bells to chime from the courthouse tower but the cost of the bells was prohibitive, and none were ever installed. The recorded chimes and programmed music emitted from the tower today are from an electronic carillon installed in 1977. The sound quality was enhanced in 1985 by the installation of larger speakers.

Anacapa Wing

The Anacapa wing of the courtrooms building to the right of the main arch contains the main lobby, information booth, and new courtrooms (departments three and four) on the main floor; the Mural Room or former supervisors' assembly room, County Clerk-Recorder's office, the court clerk's office on the second floor; and the clock tower on the fourth floor. The elections division, storage rooms, and plumbing shop are located in the basement.

On the right of the main "triumphal" arch is the smaller, but still oversized, arched entrance to the main lobby. Painted panels and a painted tympanum surround the door within this arch. To the upper left of the door is an ornate iron lantern with an

unusual winged dragon design. The twin of the dragon lantern is located nearby on the garden side of the main arch. These iron-and-glass lanterns create a sharp contrast to the rough-hewn stone behind them. Within the tunnel arch, elaborate carved stonework surrounds a second, more classically formal entry into the main lobby. The skillfully carved stone pediment and columns, as-sumed to be the designs of Cadorin, are similar to those on the façades of many Spanish buildings.

On the Anacapa Street façade, to the right of the tower, is an upper loggia/balcony outside the Mural Room (former assembly room). The "doors" that were to have open-ed from the Mural Room onto the balcony

are, however, only windows, since a miscalculation in the first floor ceiling height put the floor of the second story Mural Room lower than the bottom of the presumed doors. Inside, the resultant windows sit above a sill almost three feet high. To the right of this loggia, a staircase leading to a door with adjacent windows creates the effect of a handsome townhouse. The door no longer gives access to the building.

The little bell "tower" on the corner of the Figueroa and Anacapa street façades is a gem, in spite of its denial as a tower by the façade below it. This small and simple element, the only purely mission revival feature on the courthouse, contains the city's old fire bell. The bell was supposedly the sole survivor of a set of chimes from the clock tower of the 1896 Park Building that was destroyed in the 1925 earthquake. After the earthquake, it initially served as the fire bell for the city's former volunteer fire

department. The bell had hung on a wooden framework between the two palm trees in De la Guerra Plaza, with the fire hose beside it. When it was no longer needed by the fire department, it was decided that the fire bell would be safer in the courthouse tower.

On the sunken garden façade of the Anacapa wing, the massive main arch and tower are the major elements of the composition, as they are on the street façade, although on the garden façade the asymmetrical

placement of ornamentation makes the arch less formal and less reliant on architectural precedence. Incorporating different textures, the rough-hewn Refugio sandstone of the arch surface is edged with precisely cut square dentils. Various bas-relief sculptures, all of cast stone except for the keystone figure of Hercules, decorate the arch more or less at random. To the left of the arch, beyond a handsome grilled window, the new handicapped entrance uses a former window to give access directly into the entry hall. This new addition succeeds in its purpose without damaging the integrity of the building's original design.

Cast-Stone Decoration

The cast-stone elements on the courthouse, especially the medallions on the arch facing the sunken garden, are of uncertain origin, though two firms, Wagner & Fell and Roy Richardson, did at least some of the work. Cast stone is made from fine cement poured into a mold that is made from a sculpture. The exquisite decorative cement work on the turret of the jail tower is cast stone, as are other design elements such as corbels, water drains, cartouches, finials, window frames, grilles, and sills.

Garden Façade and Circular Stair Tower

To the upper left of the arch on the sunken garden façade of the courtrooms building is a large, cast-stone rose window, which lights the second-floor lobby. Beyond, to the left of the rose window, is a loggia echoing the loggia on the Anacapa Street façade. Both loggias are impressive in size and each loggia has segmented arches, but the thin columns of the front façade, in contrast to the low heavy posts on the garden side, make it appear higher, lighter, and airier.

The circular stair tower rising above the roofs at the interior corner of the Figueroa and Anacapa wings marks the transition between them. The tower is thought to be derived from a design by Leonardo da Vinci, who was commissioned to design such an "indoor-outdoor" tower stairwell for a chateau in the Loire Valley of France. Leonardo's design, invented as a strategic device to confuse the enemy, included two separate staircases, one located inside the other so that it was hidden from view, allowing one army to flee the building via a staircase in one direction while the opposing army climbed a staircase in another. Early twentieth-century traditionalist architect Addison Mizner often used this design feature in the Gothic-medieval-inspired Mediterranean-style houses he built in Palm Beach, Florida. Design features of the courthouse circular tower also include a circular window and a continuous series of small, beveled, round-headed windows just under the roof. On the outside of the tower a wrought-iron railing on the staircase continues with final steps to the ground. On the wall adjacent to this short flight is a grilled window, its ironwork similar to examples in *Spanish Details* by William L. Bottomly and seen in numerous houses and commercial buildings in Santa Barbara and elsewhere.

Ironwork and Other Metalwork

Metalwork found throughout the exterior of the courthouse uses traditional Spanish designs that authenticate the building's historical sources and add delightful vignettes to mitigate the plainness of the white walls. Hand-wrought iron window grilles, ornate gates, balconies, balustrades, handrails, decorative finials, door hardware, decorative studs, and shutter holders embellish the courthouse.

The most striking use of metalwork is for lighting fixtures, whether they are small sconces affixed directly onto walls, or huge elaborate lanterns hung from pendant chains or brackets. Their sturdiness and weight complement the massive buildings, and their designs and fine workmanship add dimension and idiosyncratic elements to corners, recesses, and protrusions throughout.

All metal items were specifically designed by the architects or chosen by them from catalogs to either order or copy. Fabricated in Santa Barbara and Los Angeles, the designs include heavy iron or steel balcony balustrades, handrails, and all door hardware. Copper was also used, for example, in the large exterior lanterns where it was finished to resemble wrought iron. Thin, pliable copper was intricately cut for the decorative surrounds of small wall sconces.

Traditional Spanish motifs found in architectural books that were in print at the time of construction often served as references for the metalworkers. As with the huge lanterns, prototypes for other products were found in catalogs from Spain. During that era, independent ironworkers, as well as larger metalwork firms in Los Angeles, cherished their heritage of fine workmanship and design, honoring the ideals of medieval guilds. Fortunately, the economics of the time allowed the expense of this labor-intensive industry.

Specific information as to which companies were involved in the fabrication of the courthouse's ironwork is fragmentary. Los Manos Ironworks of Santa Barbara was credited in the August 1929 *Morning Press* special edition with some of the ironwork. Also, the Earle Hardware Manufacturing Company of Los Angeles (which went out of business in 1929) has all of the courthouse's door hardware in its Catalog No.A-3 of

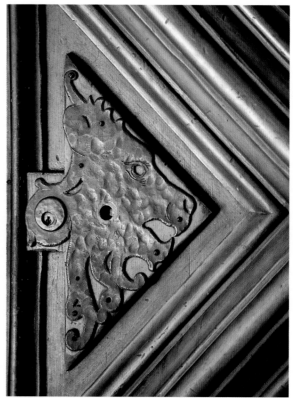

builders' hardware. One escutcheon, however, that may have been specifically designed for the courthouse is the large, ornate, double lion head surrounding the door locks of the double doors facing the law library. Gustave Schmitter of Santa Barbara made the large exterior lantern with the snake design and the pendant lamp at the entrance

to the jail. H. Dombrink Company in Oakland, California, with whose work the Mooser firm was surely familiar, fabricated and furnished the glass for many of the other lanterns. Santa Barbara resident Walter Cordero worked on the balustrades surrounding the clock tower. Other heavy-gauge ironwork, such as gates, balustrades, and handrails, was also made by local iron-workers. These companies used a particular catalog from Spain (in which many of the courthouse's lighting fixtures are pictured) and the architects' specifications for their metalwork designs. Both sources are found in the county records.

Courtrooms Building–
Figueroa Wing, Garden Façade

Viewed from the sunken garden, the court-rooms section of the Figueroa wing to the left of the circular staircase is clearly delin-eated by its higher roof and balanced façade. The expanse of white wall with a minimum of openings captures the Andalusian ideal of simplicity, especially on this rather plain façade, where the visual contrast of the landscape's palm trees and the shadows they cast are particularly effective. The entrance to this section is more impressive than the corresponding entrance on Figueroa Street (which is obscured by a loggia) because of its large size and because it is emphasized by a second doorway located on a balcony above the first. Appearing as a dark tunnel from a distance, this garden façade entrance con-tains, on its lower level, a central arched opening that is approached by steps and a spacious landing. Although the entrance is a large arch, its scale is humanized by low pilasters supporting the moldings and by extensive turned-wood grillework whose horizontal elements are at the height of an ordinary door.

The terrace, or landing, in front of the door becomes the main stage of what is, in effect, an outdoor auditorium. An auditorium was specified in the 1919 competition. With the courthouse as a backdrop, Spanish dancing during Santa Barbara's Fiestas, civic events, and community concerts are enjoyed here throughout the year.

Upon the balcony platform above the stage, approached by a pair of staircases leading upward in opposite directions from the centrally placed first-floor entrance, are benches faced with tile by Gladding, McBean. In the center of the façade, large wooden double doors that lead into the second-floor lobby are protected by an eyebrow-style tile roof supported by massive wooden corbels. The decorative tile that surrounds it and the ornate copper wall sconces on either side emphasize the doorway.

On the ground level to the left of the stage are interlacing pointed brick arches, a coloristic treatment similar to that found on the cathedral of Monreale in Sicily and on the interior of the Moorish Great Mosque of Cordoba. This is the only place in the building where brick has been used in this fashion. Besides being a unique design element, the arches are functional in that they provide light to the lower passageway of the building.

**Courtrooms Building–
Figueroa Wing, Figueroa Street Façade**
The tower-like unit that breaks through the roofline near Anacapa Street commands attention with a wide, intricately detailed cast-stone Spanish-style frieze at its cornice, corner finials, and large cartouche decorating the façade. Almost overlooked, the corner balcony on the opposite end of the building has a squat column in the angle and a stucco balustrade decorated with cast-stone floret medallions. Heavy corbels support it.

The arch that marks the main entrance to the Figueroa wing is slightly larger than the other arches of the loggia. The entrance is further emphasized overhead by the finely wrought iron balcony in front of a door opening into the law library.

Another entrance, the "lawyers' entrance," near the corner of Anacapa and Figueroa streets, also gives access to the building's main hall. Its pointed arch, made

up of a series of moldings, is similar to archivolts of Gothic cathedral doorways, although this arch is somewhat lower and wider in its proportions than its medieval precedents. The entry door is recessed within the arch and is more human in scale. An intricate metal lantern hanging within the alcove lights the entry.

In the outermost band of the moldings, a quote from *The Institutes* (1628) vol. I, by Sir Edward Coke, is inscribed: REASON IS THE LIFE OF THE LAW. The quote by the English barrister, member of Parliament, and Chief Justice of the Court of Common Pleas (head of the common-law court system) who championed the supremacy of the common law courts above all other types of English court systems, is a particularly appropriate symbol of the Anglo-American legal system.

The Jail Wing

The jail wing, found at the other terminus of the courthouse's U-shaped complex, originally housed the jail cells and jailer's apartments, but is now used for the Sheriff's office, the District Attorney's office, various administrative offices, a conference room, and temporary holding cells for prisoners. The basement contains a parking garage. The open area beyond this part of the building was planned for other buildings but was never used. The jail wing is attached to the Figueroa wing by a "bridge of sighs" walkway, an allusion to Venetian architecture, and by a curved wall at the end of the Figueroa wing corridor.

The architect used evocative, easily recognizable elements of medieval architecture to convey his vision of the dungeon tower of a castle. Most notable is his placement of a small, embellished cast-stone turret at the corner of the tower. It is similar to those found on many Spanish buildings, for example Key Tower in Salamanca, but it is completely idiosyncratic in its design. The turret with its conical roof was once used as a lookout, but is no longer safe.

Another castle reference, a gigantic, heavy, wood-grilled door with an appropriate heavy iron lock on the jail's grand main entrance on Santa Barbara Street can close off the jail as though it were a fortress. A wide, flat arch, twenty-one feet in height, surrounding the double-door is made of

proportionally large-scaled sandstone voussoirs, or wedge-shaped pieces. Carved into the arch is a Latin quote from Virgil's Aeneid: DIS CITE JUSTITIAM MONITI. The translation, "Learn justice from this warning," and its source are inscribed over a stone-framed window to the left. The ornamental, rectangular hood molding that forms an outline above the arch is especially reminiscent of that on the Casa de Doña Maria la Brava in Salamanca. As with other entrances in the building, human scale is re-established inside the entryway, here by a mock two-story façade of a Spanish-style house.

A stone path, imperceptibly sloping past the flowers and over the lawn from the sidewalk of Santa Barbara Street, leads to the main door of the jail building. It is a truly ingenious design. The path is completely unobtrusive, and because of its low grade no handrails are necessary.

On the garden façade, roofs at four different heights and a composition of arbitrarily but rhythmically placed windows of different shapes and sizes creates an effective abstract design. A stucco staircase ascending this side of the building adds a three-dimensional feature to the pattern. A shorter, newer staircase leads to a tiled seat and a new entrance.

Landscaping and the Sunken Gardens

The landscaping surrounding the courthouse complex is integral to its design and conception as a historically authentic Spanish-Mediterranean structure. The landscaping was planned with both the large scale of the building masses and their semitropical Mediterranean setting in mind. A large part of the visual effect and charm of the complex is due to the arrangement of plantings that have matured over the past seventy years, including towering trees, swaying palms, lush flowering foliage, and expanses of emerald green lawn. Even the shadows add a welcome dimension to the bright, white-walled surfaces of the buildings. The gardens are constantly enjoyed as a park by local citizens and provide a beautiful setting for weddings, performances, civic events, and festivals.

There has always been an interest in and concern for the courthouse's landscaping, from the time of the earlier building of 1875. In 1907 the grounds were a source of pride for the community with flowers, flowering bushes, pepper trees, Norway pines, and Japanese bamboo. In those days the grounds were planned and cared for by the jailer, J.O. Arkley. In 1916 Deputy Sheriff Tom Poole took charge of the grounds, and jail inmates maintained them. By 1920 there were many palm trees on the premises, and the grounds had taken on a park-like atmosphere. But the earthquake and the construction of the current courthouse made a fresh landscaping plan a necessity.

Ralph Stevens was hired to design the new gardens. Stevens was born just south of Santa Barbara, at what is now Ganna Walska Lotusland in Montecito, a large estate famous then and now for its varied and prolific gardens. Although trained on the east coast, Stevens returned west to teach at the University of California at Berkeley, and later, in 1908, to create spectacular Mediterranean gardens in Santa Barbara, including those of Casa del Herrero and the Tremaine and Peabody estates. The revision of the garden at Lotusland, based on Stevens's father's early plantings, was perhaps his most outstanding work.

In the courthouse gardens, Stevens created a Mediterranean design using tropical and subtropical plants such as varieties of imported palms, which were popularized by Addison Mizner in his Florida estates and by Bertram G. Goodhue in his design for the 1915 Panama–California Exposition.

The new courthouse gardens, completed in 1931, reflect several major landscape changes involving construction and design. Sandstone blocks excavated from the basement and foundations of the former courthouse and jail were repositioned to form the terraces of the sunken garden that symbolize the foundation plan of the former building. The large stone globes (credited to local stone cutter Arcangelo Goggia) on each of the corner entry gateposts, which defined the nineteenth-century courthouse site as well as the current one, were integrated into the new design.

The landscape design has evolved over the years, but some of the 1929 plantings remain and have fully matured. The coast redwoods at the corner of Anapamu and Santa Barbara streets and the wisteria near the District Attorney's office on the jail wing are original, although some of the

plantings have had to be removed because of damage to the building by their roots. During the time Elmer Awl was superintendent of the grounds (1955 to 1959), it was suggested that the coast redwoods (*Sequoia sempervirens*), planted in 1926, be removed, but fortunately they were not. In 1945, Henry Bauerschmidt of the county planning staff took over the planning of the courthouse garden. His enthusiasm for palms, both newly planted and original, is evident in the gardens today, where thirty-six species from twenty-one countries thrive.

In 1991–92, when the exterior of the courthouse was modified for the first time, by Charles Moore and Rex Lotery of Urban Innovations of Los Angeles and Henry Lenny of Mahan and Lenny, Architects, of

Santa Barbara, the landscaping also underwent some subtle changes. Campbell & Campbell, Landscape Architects, of Los Angeles and Santa Barbara, redesigned portions of the courthouse grounds and landscaped the handicap paths. The firm also prepared a long-term maintenance plan for the landscaping, which has been important in perpetuating the landscaping's historical appropriateness. Regula Campbell, a partner in the firm, has said about the gardens:

> Quintessentially Californian, the gardens freely draw both from the diverse traditions of [Santa Barbara's] citizens as well as the native and historical specifics of this site to

create this new design vision. In the Mediterranean custom, architecture and landscape architecture collaborate to compose exterior spaces that are as fully described as those on the interior…. In the manner of the Franciscan missions in California, the landscape building materials [supporting walls in the sunken garden] of native sandstone are locally derived, whereas the plantings represent a worldwide collection. The grounds contain examples of some of the great trees of California including giant sequoia (*Sequoiadendron giganteum*), coast redwood (*Sequoia sempervirens*), California fan palm (*Washingtonia filifera*), and Port Orford cedar (*Chamaecyparis lawsoniana*).…

To reflect the gardens' civic role, both the type and massing of the plantings is for the most part huge in scale. Trees and mass shrub plantings define exterior spaces as well as call out entries and features in the architecture. Along Anacapa Street, two towering araucaria trees, the bunya-bunya (*Araucaria bidwillii*) and the Norfolk Island pine (*A. heterophylla*), contrast their spiky dark green forms with the smooth white planes of the building walls behind them. A magnificent collection of palms is woven into the composition.

A public landscape is a living entity, which the community utilizes and enjoys in the present and holds in trust for the future. Its ongoing health bears witness to the careful guidance and stewardship of countless individuals as well as the community as a whole.

Since the courthouse is a Santa Barbara city landmark, it falls within the review jurisdiction of the Historic Landmarks Commission. As with all proposed landscaping in the historic district, approvals are based on the current list of approved plantings, those in the original planting scheme.

The Interior

REFLECTING MOORISH tradition in architecture, the relatively unadorned exterior of the Santa Barbara County Courthouse belies the glorious treasure within. Interior wall and floor surfaces gleam with colorful glazed tile and are painted in the tradition of the Renaissance, and metal lanterns with hand-blown glass evoke a feeling of old Spain, as do ornate iron gates and grilles.

The interior of the courthouse is an expression of a golden age in decorative arts that flourished in America during the late teens and twenties. The buildings of the era were enhanced by prolific use of artwork in a variety of media including painting, decorative ceramic tile-work, architectural detailing in terra cotta, carved stonework, cast stonework, hand-wrought ironwork, and copper and bronze sculpture. Because many of the artisans working in America were experienced European-trained immigrants, their works rank technically and artistically with the finest craftwork of Europe. After World War I, these skilled laborers and artisans, who fled their home countries for more opportunity and better lives, created countless pieces of art for public and private spaces throughout America.

Embellishment of the interior can be seen primarily in the courtrooms building and in the Hall of Records. The interior design creates warmth rather than the usual coldness found in many utilitarian buildings.

The main entrance lobby of the Anacapa wing, the adjacent staircase, and the second-floor landing present examples of all the artisan-crafted treasures throughout the building. Decorative multicolored tile pervades the entry area on the floor, walls, and stairs. Ornate hand-wrought iron grilles form interior gates to the hallway corridor or "gallery" beyond. Iron-and-glass lanterns hang from the ceilings. In the second-floor lobby and stairwell, paintings and decorative

the lobby area. Wall decoration and the painted trim on the massive but stout columns of the indoor-outdoor circular staircase at the elbow of the courtrooms building recreate European design motifs.

The Mural Room, however, with its completely decorated walls and ceiling, is the *pièce de résistance* of the courthouse interior. Painted walls, stenciled and gilded ceiling, paneled doors, carved wooden furniture, and embellished leather doors make it one of the most spectacular public rooms in Santa Barbara.

The exquisite, though smaller, law library, down the hall from the Mural Room on the second floor, echoes the Mural Room in its use of design features.

painted friezes and ceilings abound. Even the lobby elevator has Spanish motifs stenciled in vivid colors on its doors. Doors, counters, and furniture display intricately designed rectilinear patterns in the wood paneling.

Other areas in the courthouse use paint treatments to accent architectural features. In the center of the Figueroa wing, painted columns, soffits, ceiling, and beams define

The Mural Room

The Mural Room is the unquestionable masterpiece of the courthouse interior. The ambience of the painted murals that cover the walls, the gilt on the colorfully stenciled Moorish-inspired ceiling, the dark-stained reproductions of Spanish furniture, and the heavy iron chandeliers overpower the visitor with their magnificence.

The Mural Room was originally designed for the 1929 County Board of Supervisors as their assembly room, where members of the board presided for over thirty years. When the elder Mooser designed the room, he said to the then-chairman, Charles Leo Preisker, "Charlie, I'm going to create for you a throne room."

His regal conception was indeed realized. Today, it is used for weddings and special civic presentations.

Large, highly decorated sets of double doors provide the main entrance from the second-floor lobby at the top of the main staircase. The insides of the inner doors closest to the Mural Room are upholstered in rich brown leather and painted with a diamond pattern overlaid with a large painted ceremonial shield that represents the unification of Spain under Ferdinand V (of Aragon) and Isabella (of Castile). On the other side of these doors two painted shields hold heraldic symbols. A large upholstered area over these doors also contains the diamond pattern and a shield. The heavy, wooden outer doors are painted on both sides with stencil designs that resemble decorative tile. The exterior side, which faces the lobby, contains an impressive bolt of iron.

Inside the Mural Room, there are two other doors along the left wall. On the opposite side of the room high, draped windows open onto the loggia facing Anacapa Street. Across the front of the room is a low dais separated from the rest of the room by the original heavy, twisted ship's rope, supported at intervals by ornately wrought iron standards.

On the front dais are four secretary-cabinets, called *escritorios* (or the older word, *vargueños*), and a larger, more ornate cabinet. Originally, each of the four supervisors had one of the smaller, multi-functional pieces of furniture located at arm's length behind him as he sat at the semicircular desk-table on the elevated platform. Since these officials did not have separate offices, the moveable secretary-cabinets were used for storage of their materials and papers. The chairman, the fifth member of the board, who sat in the center position, had the larger and more mission-style piece of furniture behind him. This larger, carved cabinet, the centerpiece of the furniture on the raised platform, created a focal point for the room.

In the past, *escritorios* were common in Spanish households because of their size and usefulness. Each cabinet consists of a case-like writing table on a carved stand with a front board that folds down. If found in the house of a wealthy nobleman, it might have been embellished with inlaid silver, tortoise shell, ivory, or mother-of-pearl, but the cabinets at the courthouse are simpler, with

painted stenciling and smaller metal locks and chest bindings for decoration.

The two elaborate high-backed leather chairs also on the dais are the original judges' chairs from the two original Superior Court rooms. When the courthouse interiors were altered visually and structurally in 1964–66 to rearrange county services, these two chairs were moved to the Mural Room. The straight-backed chairs' structures are highly carved wooden frames with female figures for finials and crests in the centers of the seat backs. The leather seats and backs are embellished with tassels, decorative nail heads, embossing, and painting. These Spanish revival pieces were designed by the Mooser firm specifically for the courthouse and executed by George M. Hyde Company of San Francisco.

Seating in the Mural Room consists of

wooden frames with leather seats and backs, fastened with heavy studs. Similar pieces are found through the courthouse.

Dan Sayre Groesbeck, Muralist

Dan Sayre Groesbeck produced the wall paintings that dominate the Mural Room with their representation of Santa Barbara history. His energetic depictions of the human spirit reflect a lifelong penchant for adventure and drama that developed out of his experiences as a veteran of five wars and as a set designer for early films in Hollywood. His bold color and oversized figurative images are highly dramatic.

His birth in 1878 aboard a ship bound for San Francisco presaged Groesbeck's lifelong fascination with travel, foreign lands, and the sea. As a war painter for the *London Graphic*, he saw service in the Boxer Rebellion in China, the Russo-Japanese War, the Mexican Revolution, World War I, and the Baltic uprisings. Because of these experiences he excelled in painting military and maritime scenes. But as a Bohemian spirit, he also related to non-aristocratic town folk, recording his impressions with evocative sketches that captured the rustic and emotional core of Russian and Korean peasantry, portraying life with energy and motion.

When his coverage of wars was over, Groesbeck returned to California. Except for a brief stint in a San Francisco art school (where his work took first prize in a national contest the day after he was expelled), he was basically a self-taught artist. He worked as a billboard painter, illustrator (of books by Jack London and Joseph Conrad and stories by O. Henry), and cartoonist (in the *Los Angeles Herald*). In Santa Barbara he became part of the small artists' colony, frequently traveling to Hollywood to work in the burgeoning film industry.

Cecil B. De Mille first brought Groesbeck to Hollywood to do "advance visualizations" for his film *The Volga Boatman*. Together they developed a technique, used in all of De Mille's subsequent films, whereby hundreds of watercolor sketches were done to show set designs, costumes, and lighting effects that the film crew and staff would attempt to replicate. Although their relationship was a tumultuous one, Groesbeck and De Mille worked together and remained friends for over twenty-five years. De Mille spoke at Groesbeck's memorial service and recalls in his autobiography, "He always knew what I wanted, and he could capture character and drama in a few strokes of his brush.... " De Mille films on which Groesbeck worked included *King of Kings*, *Northwest Mounted Police*, *Samson and Delilah*, and *Reap the Wild Wind*. David O. Selznick and other directors also hired Groesbeck to work on their films.

In June of 1924, George A. Batchelder singled Dan Sayre Groesbeck out from among the artists working in Santa Barbara for a commissioned piece for the County National Bank that would present the history of Santa Barbara as a seaside city. Groesbeck agreed to undertake the painting for $1,000 plus living expenses, which totaled $800 in groceries.

The painting, "The Landing of Cabrillo," was an immediate success. Used as the cover for a national magazine, it propelled Groesbeck into international fame and demand as a muralist. His work in this genre includes rooms in California's Del

Monte Hotel, the courthouse in Portland, Oregon, the library in Ottawa, and the King Edward Hotel in Toronto. His reputation from this painting for Batchelder enabled Groesbeck to obtain the $9,000 commission to decorate the walls of the supervisor's meeting room. "The Landing of Cabrillo" now hangs opposite the entrance to the Mural Room.

Description of the Murals

The scenes covering the walls of the Mural Room reflect the interaction of influences of Groesbeck's life. His expertise in the genres of maritime seascapes and figure painting made it possible for him to depict historical events with action and immediacy through a masterful use of color, scale, and perspective. Although he took artistic license while painting and failed to do careful research, which produced some historical errors and misspellings, he more than compensated for any lack of precision by his compelling renderings.

The first wall in sequence, the rear wall (the one containing the main entry doors), contains a banner stating, "1786 Fr. Presidente Fermin de Lasuen builds the Xth Mission at Santa Barbara after the death of Fr. Junipero Serra at Carmel." The scene depicts the construction of the mission with scaffolding against an imposing mission tower with Native Americans laboring under the supervision of Father Lasuen. Although the costuming is incorrect, the scale of the tower, the beams and ladders set at irregular angles, and the motion of the laborers create a dramatic composition. Groesbeck's forged signature is found on this wall. On the day the paintings were completed, Groesbeck left for England. When he was wired to return to Santa Barbara to sign his work, he responded that someone should simply copy his signature.

The second wall, on the left side of the entry doors (opposite the windows), displays the largest of the paintings and has three inscriptions: "The Canolino Tribe bordering the Santa Barbara Channel were the most enlightened of the California Indians," "1542 Fifty years after Columbus, Juan Rodriguez Cabrillo lands at Las Canoas with the Flag of Spain," and "1602 Vth Count of Monterey sent Viscaino North, who named the Channel at Santa Barbara." The painting depicts

members of the Chumash tribe witnessing the landing of Cabrillo. The figures are larger than life and boldly outlined, with unfurled red banners waving and a Spanish galleon in the distance. Even though the Spanish costumes are incorrect for the period and Cabrillo's sailing vessel was not a galleon, the composition is still impressive.

The third wall, the front wall (the one that creates a stage for the raised platform and that faces the seating), contains two inscriptions. Near the first, "1822 California under Mexico visualizes another change in Sovereignty," a Franciscan friar with Mexican companions and a Spanish explorer (again in inappropriate *conquistador* costume) meet a group of Anglos. The second

inscription on this wall explains that it was Frémont who entered Santa Barbara to set up his headquarters and end Mexican rule: "1846 Frémont descends San Marcos Pass into the Valley of Santa Barbara." The bright sunburst with an eagle holding unfurled banners symbolizes the beginning of the American period and creates a focal point at the front of the room.

Panels on the fourth wall (containing full-length windows framed by their original deep red, heavy velvet drapes painted with golden patterns) are symbolic renderings of the leading industries that brought economic prosperity to California and Santa Barbara. The first of the panels, "Minerals," is a painting of "forty-niners" in their search for gold; the second, "Stock," shows the horse and cattle ranches found in the valleys; the third, "Agriculture," pictures laborers harvesting a crop. The romanticized symbols over the windows on this wall represent, in turn, Spain, the Franciscans, the Great Seal of the United States, the California flag (with an odd addition of a white muzzle on the grizzly bear), and an intertwined eagle with the serpent of Mexico encircled with garlands of fruit representing the bounty of the harvest.

Near the corner of the wall, on a banner, is the emphatic salute, *Salud y Pesetas* (Health and Money), and over the small door that leads to the balcony, the inscription *Gracias a Dios!* (Thanks to God!), Groesbeck's final salute to Santa Barbara and his completion of the murals.

Groesbeck employed a common design "tie-in" technique while painting the huge expanses of sky on his wall murals. A faint, repeating diamond pattern was applied to these areas in the maritime and landscape scenes. This treatment of the upper portions of the walls visually tied the heavy, ornately decorated ceiling, painted by Smeraldi, to the rest of the room. Without this melding of patterns the Smeraldi ceiling would appear to float, having no relationship to the vast expanse of sky on the wall mural beneath it. Smeraldi's and Groesbeck's painted surfaces work together as a whole.

Fortunately for Santa Barbara, the paintings that cover the walls of the forty-by-seventy-foot room were rendered on muslin that was glued to the walls. Although this process brought the inherent problems of the fabric buckling and loosening at the corners, ironically it allowed for partial restoration in 1979 after an earthquake badly cracked the walls behind the murals. Curators carefully matched the rich and vibrant blues and greens with touches of red done in a very light medium. No fixative or varnish has ever been applied. Portions of the ceiling were also restored at that time.

Although there are dissenting opinions concerning how the murals were painted, it is widely believed that they were painted in place on the walls. Groesbeck had perfected a method of projecting a smaller sketch onto a wall, thereby providing correct perspective and scale. An outline drawn from the projected image made it possible for the details to be more efficiently painted in. He and his two assistants (called strikers), wielding brushes and scrapers high up on scaffolding, supposedly completed the paintings in only four months.

Giovanni Battista Smeraldi, Artist

John B. Smeraldi, an artist who specialized in Italian Renaissance revival painting and interior design, is believed to have painted all the ceilings of the courthouse in the Mural Room, the original courtrooms, and the lobby of the Figueroa wing. He is also believed to be responsible for the decoration on the exterior beams of the main arch tunnel, in the law library, in the interior of the Hall of Records, and in various other areas throughout the courthouse.

Giovanni Battista Smeraldi (later changed to John B. Smeraldi) was born in Palermo, Italy, and as an artist's apprentice in Rome, was trained in the Renaissance style of painting and embellishment. After his immigration in 1889, his many commissions in the United States consisted of lavishly decorated ceilings in many prominent public and historic buildings. He first worked mainly on the East Coast, where his interior design work included the Blue Room of the White House and Grand Central Station in New York City.

Smeraldi moved to Los Angeles in 1921 and was commissioned by the owners of the proposed Los Angeles Biltmore Hotel to work with its architect, Earl Heitschmidt, on the design and décor of the public rooms and huge corridors. The owner-developers wanted the Biltmore to reflect the grandeur of old Spain through the formal beauty of the Renaissance style. Descriptions of the Biltmore often stated that it possessed an elegance found in many palaces and public buildings of Italy, Spain, and France, but rarely in hotels. Smeraldi brought this same sensitivity and Old World mastery to his work in the Santa Barbara Courthouse.

similar forms in Europe. The ornate decorative painting highlighted by lavish use of shiny gilt to contrast with the deep red background can be appreciated as a whole or for each individual design element. This ceiling is typical of the *Mudejar* style, a mixture of Spanish and Moorish decorative elements developed from the Christian influence on Moorish artisans working in parts of Spain under Christian domination in the thirteen and fourteenth centuries.

The repetitive patterns were applied to the beams by a traditional painting technique. A faint cartoon marked strategic points in the design from which an outline was drawn and later painted in. This is a more painstaking process than typical stenciling, using an overlaid pattern form.

Dutch-metal gilding and bronzing-powder paint were used on ceiling details, beams, and corbels to give luster. Because of a tight budget, Smeraldi was directed to use these less expensive products, but it is possible that he also used some gold leafing, which does not tarnish, since certain areas which should have tarnished by now seem

Smeraldi's other works in southern California include embellishment of the Bridges Auditorium in Claremont and the Pasadena Civic Auditorium. The main facility of the Jonathan Club in downtown Los Angeles showcased his work until the ceilings in all of the public rooms there were painted over in the mid-1980s, as were the ceilings in the Biltmore, because the decorative Dutch-metal gilt had tarnished so badly.

Smeraldi's ceiling work in the Mural Room rivals

perfectly bright. Gilding with Dutch-metal involves applying a thin leaf of a shiny metal such as bronze or copper, but not more expensive gold, to a prepared surface. The shine remains for many years, but eventually turns toward green, then black, with age. Bronzing-powder paint, a mixture of bronze powder and an adhesive, is the least expensive product of all. In the seventy years since the courthouse's completion, the Dutch-metal gilding and bronzing-powder painted surfaces have developed a patina that has changed gradually. The darkening of the luster harmonizing with the greens and reds of nearby painted surfaces causes the design to glimmer and glow. Varnish will be needed in the future to protect the paint and prohibit the Dutch-metal gilt and bronzing-powder paint from further tarnishing. In many areas, the decoration, probably

gold leaf, still shines as brightly as when it was applied seventy years ago.

The ceilings of the two original courtrooms (departments one and two) are also *Mudejar* in design. Vivid colors complement simple geometric patterns, but lack the sparkle of the shiny gold leaf and metal-gilt of the Mural Room.

In the stairwell adjacent to the Mural Room, Smeraldi's richly decorated trough ceiling is supported by arched corner squinches. The ceiling itself is considered to be inspired by the fourteenth-century synagogue, El Transito, in Toledo, Spain, but it is also reminiscent of a ceiling in the Alhambra. Along the top of the wall is a frieze of stylized palm trees similar to friezes in the Cathedral in Monreale and the Palatine Chapel in Palermo, Sicily.

In the lobby outside the Mural Room, Smeraldi has painted two Byzantine-style angels that hover above the decorated pointed arch that faces the cast-stone Romanesque rose window. This window

symbolizes a gigantic flower, with clear glass petals trimmed with red and a wide decorative border around the edges. Further decoration by Smeraldi in this area includes a wide, ornate frieze with a repetitive pattern of flowers and birds, painted ceilings, and an interlacing geometric pattern surrounding the door of the Mural Room.

Smeraldi's interpretation of other European motifs is evident in the pattern used in the circular indoor-outdoor stairwell. This pattern, similar to one in a building in Ravenna, Italy, but with the colors transposed, was painted to resemble the mosaic work of the original. The ceiling of this stairwell, enhanced by a large Spanish-style hanging lantern, is also elaborate.

Decorative work on the arches and supporting column adjacent to the circular staircase are also by Smeraldi. The colors have faded, but the muted designs are still effective. He used heraldic symbols here as

well as on the soffits, ceiling, and beam decoration of the lobby of the Figueroa wing.

The beams throughout the building are all of cement, cast in wooden frames to simulate wood surfaces because of an ordinance that prohibited the use of wood for structural elements after the 1925 earthquake. This wood texture can be seen on the interior beams as well as on those in the main arch tunnel. Many of these were painted by Smeraldi.

Although Smeraldi used a different decorative treatment and feeling from the tiled and painted interiors of the larger buildings, he designed a unique public space for the main room of the Hall of Records. Although it makes no clear stylistic

statement, the interior is charming. Inside, massive, over-scaled, painted Ionic columns, colorful, decorative stencil-type painting, evocative dark furniture, and a huge chandelier establish an atmosphere of a castle in Moorish Spain. The room was much lighter and airier before the glass skylight in the ceiling was covered over in 1965 due to leakage. A light fixture surrounding this central chandelier was added later to provide more light.

ed by Smeraldi, as were the two wall maps. The map on one wall depicts California as an island and is taken from "Map of the New World," published in 1656 by French cartographer Nicolas Sanson in *Cartes Generales*. The other is a fictional map of Santa Barbara County. Painted angels and putti hold unfurled scrolls that identify the maps. The use of tawny browns and golden tones furthers the atmosphere of antiquity.

There is no record of why the architects chose Gothic stylistic elements for the law library, but there are design precedents that help explain the choice. Moreover, there was the desire to represent the continuity of the Anglo-American legal system.

Although an English-Gothic architectural style was not used in American governmental buildings in the nineteenth century, it was used for buildings such as churches, residences, and libraries, especially law libraries, infusing the interiors with the aura of medieval English universities and religious and academic libraries.

Design elements of Gothic architecture represent God's heaven on earth. Symbolizing heavenly inspiration, the pointed, ribbed

The Law Library

The most striking features of the law library are the painted ceiling and wall decorations. As has been noted, the evocative pattern of golden stars glimmering in an immense blue sky with a border along the supporting ribs is reminiscent of medieval libraries and has a precedent in non-representational Moorish decoration. The sky and borders were paint-

vaults and their painted, starry skies resemble other designs in the libraries of great monasteries throughout England and Europe as well as in the Star Chamber of the High Court in London.

Containing over 10,000 volumes for public and law professionals' use, the law library's small but spectacular room loosely replicates some of the libraries built in monasteries and churches in Mexico during the Spanish colonial period. For example, it resembles a downscaled, less ornate version of the magnificent 50,000–volume humanities library, the Biblioteca de Palafox (c.1649), in Puebla, Mexico, one of Spain's wealthiest provinces in the seventeenth century. Similar features are found in the law library and the Puebla interior, but in Santa Barbara they are smaller in scale and less excessive. Like the Biblioteca de Palafox, in addition to a vaulted ceiling, the law library has high, carved wooden bookshelves, in this case simply decorated with scalloped borders, finely turned endpieces, and spire-like finials at the top edges and sides. Whereas the floor of the Biblioteca is tile, the floor of the law library is currently decorated with black and white sound-damping rubber "tiles." Typical heavy, Spanish provincial furniture, such as refectory tables and straight-backed wooden chairs, is found in each of the libraries. In the law library, floor-to-ceiling windows with gold-toned paint patterned on heavy, red-velvet curtains allow natural light into the room, lending a calming atmosphere, while decorative iron chandeliers of different designs bear the much-needed sources of additional light.

Cast stonework over and around the exterior of the entrance incorporates a sword of justice, in this case the curved Moorish scimitar, with the scales of justice. Historically, a straight sword would have been represented in stone, but curving it and turning it into a scimitar was, perhaps, another Mooser nod to Moorish antecedence of the Spanish style of the building. The bas-relief of an open book in the middle of the framed piece denotes the library within.

Tile

The most striking decorative feature in the interior of the courthouse is the use of tile throughout. The tile flooring contrasted with the plain white walls is the major unifying feature of the building. The decorative tile on the surfaces of the first- and second-floor lobbies characterizes the building as Spanish. Moorish motifs on the tiles were derived from the Islamic countries of Persia and Turkey.

Spurred by the success of the 1915 Panama–California Exposition in San Diego, architects in California began to incorporate tile into their Mediterranean-style buildings, enhancing both the buildings and their gardens with a sense of the romantic and exotic. Tile companies such as Gladding, McBean and Company proliferated throughout the West Coast, and the Rossman Corporation became active in importing Spanish and North African decorative tiles. Gladding, McBean and Company, in their catalog "Tile: Tropico Faience Decorative Floors," states with enthusiasm: "Decorative Faience Tile...represents the most fugitive and eagerly sought after element in the architectural field; that of a permanent and beautiful means of flat wall embellishment."

The choice of glazed tiles to decorate the interior of the courthouse was a wise one. Not only are the tiles strikingly beautiful, but they evoke the imagery and ambiance of a Moorish–Spanish palace. Tile was a more economical wall surfacing material than granite or marble at that time. It was lightweight, cost-effective, durable, fireproof, and easily maintained. Furthermore, tile is the best product for interior ornamentation because of its versatility of color, texture, and design. It also appealed to architects because it was handmade, as were other products ornamenting the building.

Chemla Tile

The Anacapa Street entrance lobby is replete with colorful tiles created by Jacob Chemla. They cover the magnificent stairway walls, stair risers, and landing bench, as well as the window bench, the outline of the interior arches, and the wainscoting on the walls of the first floor. The small, specially designed heraldic pieces used as insets in between the larger floor tiles are also attributed to Chemla. These symbols include castles, lions, ravens, pomegranates, checkerboards, shields, and ships.

Tile wainscoting surrounds the second-floor lobby. The beauty of the staircase leading to the third floor equals that of the main staircase with its complete facing in tile and its tiled landing seat. The strikingly vibrant black-and-cream abstract geometric pattern and sunbursts complement the floral patterns. There are also two murals of vases with tree-of-life flowers, as well as some birds. Islamic artistic tradition requires a strict adherence to non-representational geometric shapes but permits floral and vegetal designs.

Chemla tile was a familiar product in Santa Barbara, having been used by architect George Washington Smith. For George Fox Steedman and his Casa del Herrero estate in Montecito, Smith located this tile manufactured in Tunis (French Tunisia). Perhaps the Mooser firm found out about the tile and its United States distributor, Rossman, from Smith.

Les Fils de Chemla

In the latter part of the nineteenth century, as interest in the restoration of ancient buildings gained momentum, Jacob Chemla, owner and operator of Les Fils de Chemla, a pottery factory in French Tunisia, was approached by the architect working on the restoration of the Persian Palais du Bardo to duplicate historic tile patterns. Because Chemla's interest was piqued by these patterns, he not only reproduced designs for tiles to restore that project, but also devoted the rest of his life to reviving the ancient art of the Persians in his factory in North Africa.

Products from Les Fils de Chemla included the traditional brightly colored glazed *azulejos* (tiles) in shades of blue, green, deep blackish brown, creamy white, and golden yellow. These tiles were made in the ancient method, in which every step of the process was painstakingly done by hand. Clay was collected from nearby Soukra and fired in kilns converted from old ovens. Stoked with slow-burning olivewood, the kilns used a direct flame to fire the glazed tiles. During the firing process, a primitive technique was used to separate the stacked tiles to insure that the glazes did not touch: Three small rounded dabs of clay were applied directly onto each tile; when the clay dabs were knocked off after the tiles had been fired, tiny remnants (pips) remained on the surface, testifying to the carefully hand-made manufacturing method.

Members of the Chemla family have continued their craft to this day. The Chemla factory relocated to Paris after World War II, and, as of 1997, is owned and operated by Andre Chemla, grandson of Joseph Chemla. The company is active in the production of the same fine decorative tile designs that it has made for over one hundred years. The architects of the courthouse were very fortunate to be able to obtain Chemla tile when they did, because during the Great Depression of the 1930s Chemla was no longer distributed in the United States.

Gladding, McBean Tile

The Mooser firm specified Gladding, Mc-Bean tile for the flooring of the first- and second-level lobbies and corridors, risers on the circular stairwell, the decorative eight-pointed Moorish star in the supervisors' seal on the first floor at the Figueroa Street entry, the tiles surrounding the interior and exterior of the huge double doors facing the entrance to the law library on the second floor, the benches on the landing in front of those doors, and the larger flooring pieces in the second-floor Mural Room. The tile patterns used from the Gladding, McBean catalog included "Fallston," "Palacio," and "Promenade," as well as some smaller decorative and colorful, or *faience*, pieces which are quite distinct from Chemla tiles.

Fallston tiles are used on all floors and stair treads throughout the first floor. They are deep in tone, browns mixed with tans and tans with a peach cast, all flecked with deeper, natural terra-cotta hues. Each floor is laid with a different pattern. Also, the lobby area on the second floor directly outside the Mural Room contains Fallston tile with smaller inset pieces of decorative Chemla tile.

The burnt red-orange Palacio tiles of the main corridors on both the first and second floors have uneven surfaces, giving an overall flowing, rippling effect to the large expanses. They seem to glow in the dimly lit hallways, giving the impression of well-maintained antique flooring. Basic eight-inch-square pieces are offset with smaller, variously shaped pieces set in a seemingly random pattern of decorative colored tiles from Chemla, primarily in shades of pale yellow and blue with backgrounds of red and green. In the large surface areas to be covered, the random use of the insets adds interest to potentially monotonous spaces.

The floor of the Mural Room contains burnt-red Promenade tile and specially designed Gladding, McBean tile as accents. These special tiles contain recessed designs that hold bright blue, white, and yellow glazes. This technique of pressing designs into wet clay and filling the recesses with glaze is called the *cuenca* method. A clear pattern is produced because the raised edges of the design prevent the glazes from running together. The tile is difficult to maintain, however, because the slight glazed indentions collect dirt as well as built-up wax and acrylic finishes, which darken with time. The floor's first thorough cleaning in 1992 led to the discovery of the brilliant accent colors and the warm red of the original tiles.

Gladding, McBean's *faience* tile in different patterns, made in the *cuerda seca* method, serves as risers in the massive, three-story circular stairwell. The *cuerda seca*, or dry line, method involves drawing outlines of the design with a compound of grease and iron oxide. The interior of the design is then filled in with different colored glazes, the greasy lines segregating the colors during firing.

Gladding, McBean and Company

Gladding, McBean and Company, formed in 1875 near Sacramento, California, was the leading manufacturer of architectural and decorative terra cotta on the West Coast by the time the Santa Barbara County Courthouse was designed. Although it was one of forty-eight competing manufacturers in the United States, its products continually garnered awards for their technical and artistic superiority, and the business had an excellent reputation among leading architects of the day.

Founded on the production of utilitarian terra cotta products such as sewer pipe, water pipe, and chimney caps, Gladding, McBean expanded into other areas with the enthusiasm for terra cotta decoration on urban buildings. Steel-framed skyscrapers needed to be faced, and terra cotta provided an excellent product. Compared to hand-carved stone, it was readily available in large units, could be transported efficiently, functioned as a fire-proof curtain wall, was less expensive because it was less labor-intensive, and could be made to simulate stone, including granite and marble. Huge

architectural projects from this era in major West Coast cities are clad with Gladding, McBean terra cotta, and often the interiors are decorated with fine, colorful, glazed tile.

Decorative tiles for use in the courthouse came from Tropico Potteries in Glendale, California, a subsidiary of Gladding, McBean. With purchase of this facility in the 1920s Gladding, McBean had expanded its sphere of influence into the ever-increasing demand for small decorative terra cotta products, including glazed tile. From the mid 1910s through the 1920s, the popular use of terra cotta to ornament buildings was at its height. With the advent of the Great Depression of the 1930s, terra cotta was no longer used on a grand scale.

Ironically, because of its original products, Gladding, McBean has weathered the waning use of terra cotta for architectural ornamentation by continuing to produce its utilitarian products. It is the only company left today from that golden era. Although it does not survive on commissions for its ornamental products, a variety of them are still available, made from the original molds and glazed in colors made from the original formulas.

La Fitte Tile

The three large tiles, each depicting a seated female figure, and the floral patterned border tiles surrounding them located on the buttresses of the stairways in both the first- and second-story lobbies are attributed to the Spanish company La Fitte, produced by José La Fitte. The border tiles surrounding the mosque mural on the main staircase landing are also by La Fitte, as are, possibly, some inset tiles in the second-floor lobby. These tiles are different in appearance from those of Gladding, McBean, with less distinct patterns and a "washed out" look. The Rossman Corporation imported this tile as well as that of Chemla. Contrary to commonly held opinion, Batchelder-Wilson Company products were not used in the courthouse.

New Tile

From time to time, the courthouse has required the use of new tile. Copies of Gladding McBean "Palacio" tiles, called "Barcelona" by the manufacturer, were used in the 1991 construction of the interior ramp between the jail and Figueroa wings. Ceramic artist Judith Sutcliffe produced the smaller tiles for the decorative insets. Architect Jack Dewey designed the star pattern on the floor inside the ramp, and the tiles for it were hand painted by Ann Sacks of Oregon.

Sutcliffe also made the tiles surrounding the first-floor drinking fountains. A fifteen-foot section of red tiles was replaced in the assembly wing first-floor gallery because of damage in 1987. There, unbroken decorative "Palacio" Gladding, McBean tiles were carefully preserved from that location and later combined with copies by Viqui McCaslin at Coyote Kilns in Ojai for use in reconstructing the floor.

Tile Plaques

Similar to the plaques on the exterior of the Hall of Records and in the entrance tunnel are two tile plaques on interior walls. The one located to the left of the main lobby elevator recognizes the contribution of George A. Batchelder, civic leader, to the construction of the building. In the plaque, a soft cream-colored background holds burnt brownish-reddish-orange lettering framed in a multicolored border with scrollwork and classical figures. It is unsigned and the maker is unknown.

A tile plaque on the wall of the second-floor assembly gallery facing the sunken gardens uses shades of green and brown, appropriate to its indoor-outdoor setting. A tree-lined country road serves as a background for the script honoring brothers George and Charles Edwards, community benefactors. It is a gift from the Edwards family. This also is an unsigned work.

The most impressive tile plaque in the courthouse is inset into the floor where the corridors of the two wings of the courtrooms building meet. This mosaic depicts the Board of Supervisors' insignium surrounded by a large eight-pointed Moorish star. Made with Gladding, McBean tile, the star's three borders begin with an outer strip of deep, sea-blue tile, then move inward with a terra cotta and white design of a pine-and-palm motif, followed by an inner border of burnt orange. The center holds a castle tower,

which can be found on the old seal of the Board of Supervisors. A chalice is centered on top of this with stylized bolts of lightning shooting forth. At the base of this picture, a pale-blue sea area holds classical representations of dolphins frolicking between waves, symbolizing Santa Barbara's proximity to the ocean. The castle tower and bolts of lightning represent the legend of Saint Barbara, who was imprisoned in a tower by her father after converting to Christianity. When she did not renounce her faith, he executed her and was in turn struck by lightning.

A bronze medallion honoring the Native Sons of the Golden West, surrounded by a crisscrossed tile pattern, is located at the base of the circular indoor-outdoor stairwell. The molded-bronze medallion holds a bas-relief of California's symbol, the grizzly bear, encircled by the dedication date of August 14, 1929 and the name of the donor, the Native Sons of the Golden West.

This plaque was laid following an elaborate ceremony on August 14, 1929. On an outdoor stage before a large crowd all of the supervisors mixed sand, gravel, cement, and water as they explained the significance of each element. The sand and gravel, gathered from each county in the state of California represented its natural resources; the cement, collected from various manufacturing plants in the state, represented industry; and the water, collected from each of the twenty-one California Missions, represented tradition. Immediately following this ceremony the cement mixture was carried to the interior site and used in setting the plaque.

The Corridors

Each of the four major passageways through the L-shaped courtrooms building presents an individual ambience. Down the dimly lit first-floor gallery of the Anacapa wing, wide, flattened arches rhythmically break up the vista and minimize the effect of the height of the passageway. The corridor above on the second floor is flooded in light by the open loggia facing the garden.

The well-defined entrance lobby interrupts the first-floor corridor of the Figueroa wing. On the second floor, high, draped windows light the gallery. As on the first floor, its length is broken in the center, in this instance by the entrance to the law library and the large door from the garden.

Doors

Doors throughout the courthouse, many made of solid oak or walnut, are richly designed with geometric patterns created by raised moldings. Leather-covered doors with their heavy nails, known as *clavos* or bosses, and doors with decorative wooden spindles are artworks in themselves. The same type of elaborate molding used on some of the doors has been incorporated as decorative treatment for desks and counters in various offices in the building.

The doors leading to Superior Court rooms one and two were originally faced with leather padding, but because of bad buckling and cracking problems the leather was removed in 1994. The padded and studded leather surfaces were authentically reproduced in a more durable, dark brown vinyl material, and the doors were completed, as before, with brass studs.

Spindled doors similar to those on the Figueroa wing entrances can be found throughout Spain and Morocco. The divisions in these doors and the size of the spindles bring the doors to a more human scale for those entering the building. Another unusual door with small wooden spindles in its upper lunette is located in the doorway leading into the service building from the main arch tunnel.

In other areas of the courthouse, various metal doors have been treated to simulate traditional styles. The elevator doors (Forderer Cornice Works, San Francisco) in the main lobby and near the circular stairwell display typical Spanish motifs of repetitive geometric patterns in paint.

Furniture

Throughout the corridors much of the furniture appears as sculpture. The furniture is functional and durable, designed and built with the historical context of the building in mind. The use of authentic materials such as wood, leather, and iron, with embellishments of carved and painted ornamentation, adds charm and warmth rarely found in public buildings. The furniture was designed for the courthouse under the direction of William Mooser III and was executed by the interior design firms of Alfred Vezina Building & Construction and George M. Hyde Company of San Francisco. County records state that these firms were responsible for the carpets, leatherwork, hangings, drapes, ornamental hardware, and furniture fittings as well. They also executed the millwork of the wooden elements of the courthouse, which includes doors, railings, and grilles.

Many of the courthouse furniture pieces have their design precedent in domestic and public interiors of sixteenth- and seventeenth-century provincial Spain. The furniture, not known for elegance or a high degree of craftsmanship but for strength and substantial quality, has been described as masculine, simple, and strong, with straight-backed chairs and benches, or

chairs upholstered with taut leather seats.

The courthouse contains many reproduction pieces that define Spanish décor, such as tables, chairs, benches, chests, and secretary-cabinets. Chairs have carved heraldic escutcheons in the center backs and sturdy leather seats decorated with metal studs and iron cross-ties between the legs. Benches are equally Spanish in their design.

All of the furniture in the courthouse is made of either oak or walnut, and some pieces from the previous nineteenth-century courthouse were refurbished, probably by L.B. Nolley, as an economical consideration.

Paintings

Paintings hung throughout the courthouse turn the corridors into galleries and add another dimension to the interior with their visual representations of a romantic Spanish past for the courthouse. Except for the work by Channing Peake, the paintings, all completed during the twenties, were commissioned and donated by community benefactors and painted by Allan Gilbert Cram, Della Shull Thompson Rich, and Theodore Van Cina.

Three paintings by Allan Gilbert Cram (1886–1947) hang in the first-floor lobby and tiled stairway. The first, entitled "Spanish Horseman on a Palomino Horse," inspired by and honoring Dwight Murphy (Montecito rancher and one of Santa Barbara's most important philanthropists) shows a gentleman in the traditional Spanish regalia of a *caballero* (gentleman cowboy) on a rearing horse. The silver-accented saddle and golden Palomino were Murphy's trademarks as he rode in many Fiesta parades. Santa Barbara landmark buildings, such as the Lobero Theatre, the mission, and St. Anthony's Seminary, form parts of the foreground and background. The painting was commissioned and given to the county by Max Fleischmann, another important community philanthropist.

The second painting, a full-length portrait entitled "The Cowman" was inspired by, but probably not posed for, by Ed Borein, once a working cowboy and a fellow Santa Barbara painter in the "western" genre. The painting portrays a working cowboy rustically costumed with leather chaps, hat, and vest. Cram often used the technique of painting a smaller picture

within the larger one: the loop formed by the cowman's lariat contains a colorful ranching scene of horses. The third painting, "Spanish Woman in Red," a striking portrait of a seated woman, shows a *señora* wearing a deep-red Spanish dress with a dramatically contrasting black-and-floral shawl and an elaborate headdress. The figure represents the upper-class fondness for fine clothing even in the nineteenth century frontier town of Santa Barbara.

Although born in Washington D.C., Cram grew up in the seafaring towns of New Bedford, Gloucester, and Marblehead,

Massachusetts, and considered himself a New Englander. At fourteen he began studying art seriously and by age eighteen had exhibited his work in New York. Formal training consisted of sessions at the Art Students' League in New York and classes with William Merritt Chase. He traveled for several years in Italy and became a member of the famous art colony of Ogunquit, Maine. On a trip to the West Coast to visit an uncle who owned the Del Valle-Camulos Ranch in Santa Paula, Cram decided to settle in Santa Barbara. He bought a ranch in Goleta, a few miles north, and became a well-known member of the Santa Barbara artist colony during the 1920s and 30s. He worked out of studios first on Laguna Street, then on the mesa hillside area of Santa Barbara, and finally on Hillcrest Road, where he later resided.

Cram is known not only for his western genre paintings, but also for his maritime works and seascapes, which show his passion for the sea in all its moods and his knowledge of sailing vessels. Many of his works are displayed in public buildings in Santa Barbara, including the Rockwood Women's Club and the Santa Barbara Yacht Club. A selection of his pencil sketches may be found at Stanford University.

Two large paintings by Della Shull Thompson Rich (1878–1961) hang in the courthouse. They are full-length portraits, one of a man and the other of a woman, both standing in formal poses. Della's first husband, New York attorney Kennedy Thompson, posed for the portrait entitled "Gentleman in Spanish Dress" wearing a typical costume for an upper-class gentleman, an elegant black suit trimmed in red

braid and delicate black slipper shoes. "Lady in a White Gown" exhibits the elegance of a beautiful, floor-length, white-lace dress with highly contrasting black lace *mantilla* (shawl) worn over a *peineta* (hair comb) and fashionable red shoes.

Like Cram, Rich studied painting with William Merritt Chase and Robert Henri in New York. Her earlier studies abroad had led her to Spain and France, where she had become a member of the art colony at Fontainebleau. After living in New York, she settled in Santa Barbara during the 1930s, where she had a studio in the artists' colony situated downtown near De la Guerra and Garden streets. During her lifetime her paintings sold well and she was famous for her treatment of hands. It is not known what happened to her collection, as she died a widow in 1961 without heirs.

The third artist, Theodore Van Cina, was a Dutch painter, sculptor, and teacher who studied at the Academy of Fine Arts, Rotterdam, and traveled widely in Europe studying medieval art. He explained that the reason for his move to California in 1924 was "to aid in the revival of the early Spanish spirit in California painting." The classical style of his three paintings in the courthouse contrasts with the painterly style of Groesbeck.

During his short stay in Santa Barbara, from 1929 to 1930, Van Cina was commissioned by Fred D. Jackson of Mortgage Securities, Inc., of Santa Barbara to paint six large (eight by sixteen feet) historical paintings that would be unveiled as part of Fiesta week celebration. Originally painted for an office building, they were lost to the public for many years, stored in the basement of a hotel where they had once hung. In 1964,

the new owner of the building recovered them and offered them to the county. Through the efforts of former Supervisor Joe Callahan, three of them now hang in the upper galleries of the courthouse. These historical paintings, each a colorful, elaborate mural that recounts a story from Santa Barbara's past, are "El Fandango a la Casa de la Guerra" (The Dance at the De la Guerra Home), "El Pirata Bouchard Pillando el Rancho Refugio" (The Pirate Bouchard Pillages the Rancho Refugio), and "El Desembarco de Cabrillo a Santa Barbara" (The Landing of Cabrillo at Santa Barbara).

"El Fandango," a popular favorite among the three paintings, shows a lively party held in the courtyard of the Casa de la Guerra, the mansion-home of the wealthy José de la Guerra that served as the social center of Santa Barbara. Known as the patriarch of the town, José de la Guerra sits in a place of honor with a priest, enjoying dancers and a band, along with many guests. As comandante of the presidio from 1815 to 1842, De la Guerra enjoyed a reputation for generous hospitality that was well known throughout Alta California. Visitors to his home, such as Richard Henry Dana, were royally entertained there. A wedding at the Casa de la Guerra in 1836 is recounted in Dana's *Two Years Before the Mast.*

"El Pirata" depicts the triumphant pirate, Hipolito Bouchard, with prisoners and treasure from the pillaged Rancho del Refugio, north of Santa Barbara. (Actually, Rancho del Refugio was warned early enough for the inhabitants to escape with their valuables, but the ranch buildings were destroyed and cattle killed.) Sailing under the Argentine flag, opposing Spanish rule wherever he found it, Bouchard's raids on Spanish colonization efforts along the California coast began when he and his 350 men, sailing in two vessels from the Sandwich Islands (Hawaii), attacked and ransacked Monterey, the capital of Alta California. Soon thereafter, in 1818, he sailed south toward Del Refugio, one of the largest and richest ranches in Santa Barbara County, where meager efforts of *soldados* from the fort could not prevent destruction of the buildings. Satisfied with his terrorization of Spanish California after he sacked and burned San Juan Capistrano, Bouchard returned to South America, where he founded the Argentine Navy.

"El Desembarco de Cabrillo" shows members of the Chumash tribe greeting Juan Rodriguez Cabrillo, the first European to land at what was to become Santa Barbara. Cabrillo's two grand ships are depicted as galleons, similar to those in the painting of the same subject by Dan Sayre Groesbeck in the second-floor lobby, when in fact Cabrillo's ships were considerably less impressive.

Van Cina's other three paintings in this series, "El Padre Serra Plantando la Cruz para el Presidio" (Father Serra Planting the Cross at the Presidio), "El Funeral del Gobernador José Figueroa" (The Funeral of Governor José Figueroa), and "El Encumbrimiento del Cañón Perdido" (The Hiding of the Lost Cannon) are scattered throughout Santa Barbara.

In 1999, the county hung a large mural depicting the Old Spanish Days Fiesta in the Figueroa wing of the courthouse. Painted by Channing Peake, it was originally commissioned in 1984 by the Santa Barbara Trust for Historic Preservation to decorate the Gold Room of the El Paseo restaurant. When the trust sold the El Paseo, the mural was given to the county.

Channing Peake (1910–1989) attended both the Oakland School of Arts and Crafts and the Santa Barbara School of Art. In the mid 1930s, he painted murals with Diego Rivera in Mexico. He studied with Rico LeBrun at the Art Students League and worked with him on the murals in Pennsylvania Station in New York. He lived for many years in the Santa Ynez Valley.

Postscript

THE SANTA BARBARA COUNTY COURTHOUSE stands today as a unique monument of architectural brilliance in California, and it is the prized jewel of the city and county whose people it serves and whose visitors it delights.

What makes it so are the myriad contributions of a host of skilled architects, designers, artisans, and craftsmen in a variety of media—the individuals and companies described in this book—whose talents were expressed in the kind of traditional handwork that is seldom seen nowadays.

From the foundation up, the courthouse builds upon tradition with a stunning individuality. It is steeped in the traditions of Spain and Old California, infused by the worldwide revival of arts and crafts of the 1900s to 1920s, and inspired by a style and spirit all its own. It not only reflects Santa Barbara's image of itself, but has greatly influenced that image as well. Viewed from any angle, inside or outside, on scales large or small, the Santa Barbara County Courthouse never ceases to delight. Thus it remains as refreshingly beautiful today as it was when it was built three quarters of a century ago, and no doubt visitors will still find it so many generations hence.

Bibliography

Architectural Advisory Committee. Financial Report, July 1925–January 1926.

"Bank of Montecito, Historic Facility Opens." *Santa Barbara News-Press* (January 28, 1979).

Barrucand, Marianne and Achim Bednorz. *Moorish Architecture in Andalusia*. Cologne: Rolf Taschen, 1992.

Bartlett, John. *Familiar Quotations*. Boston: Little, Brown and Company, 1901.

Battu, Zoe A. "Ornamental Tile—Its History and Renaissance." *Pacific Coast Architect*. Vol. 31 (May 1927): 49.

Bauerschmidt, Henry. Interview. December 2, 1993.

Bottomly, William Lawrence. *Spanish Details*. New York: William Helburn, Inc., 1924.

Byne, Arthur and Mildred Stapley. *Spanish Interiors and Furniture*. New York: William Helburn, Inc., 1921–22.

Cadorin, Ettore. "Monumental and Decorative Statuary." *California Southland*. Vol. 10 (January 1928):13, 26.

Chase, Pearl. "Bernhard Hoffmann—Community Builder." *Noticias*. Vol. 5 (Summer, 1959): 15–24.

"Civic Leaders Urge Unique Architecture." (Santa Barbara) *Morning Press* (July 9, 1925): 3.

Cleek, Patricia Gardner. "Santa Barbara Stone Masonry." *Noticias*. Vol. 10 (Spring, 1994):1–24.

"Competition for Santa Barbara County Court House and Memorial." *The Building Review.* Vol. 18 (November, 1919): 85–93.

"Contracts to be Awarded in Several Units." (Santa Barbara) *Morning Press* (October 4, 1925).

"County Favors Auditorium in Court House." (Santa Barbara) *Morning Press* (July 10, 1925).

"County Will Set Courthouse Bond Election Nov. 17." (Santa Barbara) *Morning Press* (October 4, 1925).

"Court Design Row Given to Noted Group." (Santa Barbara) *Morning Press* (Sept. 19, 1925): Sect. 2, p.1.

"Court House Competition." *Southwest Builder and Contractor.* Los Angeles, California. Whole Number 1374: Vol. 54: no. 4 (July 25, 1919).

"Courthouse Bond Call Will Follow Receipt of Plans." (Santa Barbara) *Morning Press* (April 17, 1926).

"Courthouse Competition." *Southwest Builder and Contractor* (July 25, 1919).

"Courthouse has Roots in the Past." *Santa Barbara News-Press* (July 31, 1977): 37, 39.

"Courthouse Plans Given Unanimous Endorsement by Advisory Committee." (Santa Barbara) *Morning Press* (April 11, 1926).

Cram, Mildred. "Allan Gilbert Cram." *Encino Community News* (December 1, 1941): 4–5.

De Mille, Cecil B. *The Autobiography of Cecil B. De Mille.* Englewood Cliffs, New Jersey: Prentice-Hall, Inc., 1959.

Finney, M. Mac Leon. "The Court House Beautiful." *Architect and Engineer.* Vol. 98 (July, 1929): 35–46.

Gebhard, David and Harriette Von Breton. *Architecture in California* 1868–1968. Santa Barbara, California: The Art Galleries, University of California, Santa Barbara, April 1968.

Gebhard, David. *Santa Barbara—The Creation of a New Spain in America.* Santa Barbara, California: University Art Museum, November 1982.

Goodrich, Jean Smith. "Tile at the Casa del Herrero." *Noticias.* Vol. 42 (Autumn 1996): 59–61.

"Guidelines: El Pueblo Viejo District, Santa Barbara, California." Santa Barbara, California: City of Santa Barbara, 1995.

"The Hall of Records: A Beautiful County Building Just Completed." *The Daily Independent*, Santa Barbara (Sept 11, 1889): 4.

Hayes, Marjorie. "The Tiles of the Santa Barbara Courthouse." *Noticias*. Vol. 42 (Autumn 1996): 54–58.

Hogue, Fred S. "Dan Sayre Groesbeck." *Los Angeles Times* (February 10, 1924).

Jackman, Jarrell C. *Santa Barbara: Historical Themes & Images.* Norfolk, Virginia: The Donning Company Publishers, 1988.

Kurutz, Gary F. *Architectural Terra Cotta of Gladding, McBean.* Sausalito, California: Windgate Press, 1989.

Laws, Bill. *Traditional Houses of Rural Spain.* New York: Abbeville Press, 1995.

Little, Ruth. "County Law Library is Busy Place." *Santa Barbara News-Press* (April 13, 1959).

Mayer, August L. *Old Spain.* New York: Brentano's, 1921.

McMahon, Marilyn. "Accent on Landscaping and Access." *Santa Barbara News-Press* (March 5, 1992): D 4.

"Million Will be Expended on Structure." (Santa Barbara) *Morning Press* (July 4, 1925): Sect. 2, p.1.

Minutes. Meeting of General Architectural Advisory Committee (July 7, 1925).

Moore, Charles. "Plug It in, Rameses, and See if It Lights Up, Because We Aren't Going to Keep it Unless it Works." *Perspecta.* Vol. 11 (1967): 32–43.

Moore, Charles. "Action Architecture: The Santa Barbara County Courthouse and Le Corbusier's Carpenter Center," in *Dimensions: Space, Shape & Scale in Architecture.* New York: Architectural Record Books, 1976. p. 41–50.

"Mooser Again Retained for Drawing Plan." (Santa Barbara) *Morning Press* (January 5, 1926).

Mooser, William. "Building of Court House Within Architect's Estimate." *Architect and Engineer.* Vol. 98 (July 1929): 47, 83.

Mooser, William. "Sketches and the Model for the Court's Hall of Records and Dungeon Tower." *California Southland.* Vol. 10 (January, 1928): 11.

"New Courthouse Will be the First Distinctive Monumental Building: Plans for County Offices Approved by Board Members." (Santa Barbara) *Morning Press* (September 27, 1925).

"New Santa Barbara Courthouse as Approved by Advisory Board." (Santa Barbara) *Morning Press* (April 11, 1926).

Newcomb, Rexford. *Spanish-Colonial Architecture in the United States.* New York: Dover Publications, Inc., 1990 (reprint of 1937 publication).

Newcomb, Rexford. *Architectural Monographs on Tiles and Tilework.* No. 7. New York: Associated Tile Manufacturers, 1929.

"Notes and Comments," *Architect and Engineer.* Vol. 59 (November 1919): 113–114.

O'Dowd, Patrick. "Pirate Outwitted! Santa Barbara Saved!" *Santa Barbara Magazine* (Winter 1998): 64–68.

O'Neill, Owen. *History of Santa Barbara County.* 1939.

Palmer, Kevin. "Courting the Civic Image." *Noticias.* Vol. 37 (Spring 1991): 1–11.

Reid, Richard. *The Book of Buildings: A Panorama of Ancient, Medieval, Renaissance, and Modern Structures.* Chicago, New York, San Francisco: Rand McNally & Company, 1980.

Rouse, Stella Haverland. "Earthquake Precipitated Need for New Courthouse." *Santa Barbara News-Press* (July 29, 1979): 39–44.

Rouse, Stella Haverland. "The Way It Was." *Santa Barbara News-Press* (Sunday, May 1, 1988).

Ruskin, John. *The Stones of Venice.* Vol. I. New York: E.P. Dutton & Co., 1921.

"Sam Doesn't Want a Cent Out of Fund." (Santa Barbara) *Morning Press* (December 11, 1928).

Santa Barbara Architecture from Spanish Colonial to Modern. Santa Barbara: Capra Press, 1995.

Santa Barbara County Board of Supervisors. Minutes. Various dates.

"Santa Barbara County Courthouse." (Santa Barbara) *Morning Press*, Fiesta Edition (August 14, 1929).

"The Santa Barbara County Court House." Santa Barbara, California: Board of Supervisors, 1929.

"Santa Barbara Court House Competition." *Architect and Engineer*. Vol. 56 (February 1919): 109.

(Santa Barbara) *Morning Press* (July 18, 1925; July 25, 1925; September 5, 1925; September 26, 1925; January 5, 1926; October 24, 1928; November 5, 1928; November 21, 1928; November 30, 1928; January 3, 1929; February 6, 1929; February 7, 1929.

Sordo, Enrique. *Moorish Spain*. New York: Crown Publishers, Inc., 1963.

Soule, Winsor. *Spanish Farm Houses and Minor Public Buildings*. New York: Architectural Book Publishing Co., 1924.

"Supervisors Vote to Leave Details to Citizens Group." (Santa Barbara) *Morning Press* (February 20, 1926).

"Terra Cotta: Past to Present." *Architectural Record* (January 1987): 110–113.

Tompkins, Walker A. *Santa Barbara Past and Present: An Illustrated History*. Santa Barbara, California: Schauer Printing Company, Inc., 1975.

"Three Story Court Asked." (Santa Barbara) *Morning Press* (September 9, 1925).

Whitehead, Richard S. "A History of the Santa Barbara County Court House." City of Santa Barbara Landmarks Committee Staff Report. Santa Barbara (Jan. 27, 1982).

Whittlesey, Austin. *The Minor Ecclesiastical, Domestic and Garden Architecture of Southern Spain*. New York: Architectural Book Publishing Co., 1917.

"The Young Architect and the New Town." *California Southland*. Vol. 10 (December, 1928): 16–17.